# WITHOUT A VOICE

To Jennifer

# Without A Voice

*A Woman's Journey to Resiliency*

**ERIKA OBANDO**

*Edited by ExpertCopy*

Erika Obando

Paperback Edition ISBN: 978-0-578-79180-7
eBook Edition ISBN 978-0-578-79800-4
Without A Voice - A Woman's Journey to Resiliency/Memoir/Inspirational

Front cover design by Ekechi Pitt
www.EkechiPitt.MyPortfolio.com
Back cover design by Cristian Chavez
www.CristianChavezMedia.com
Cover photography by Eugenio Wilman & Daniuska Lambert
www.TheWeddingTraveler.com;
Cover wardrobe by Amanda Perna
www.TheHouseofPerna.com;
Cover hair and makeup by Gina Dearing
www.GinaDearing.com
Edited by: ExpertCopy
Printed and Bound in the United States of America
Distribution (Worldwide): IngramSpark

First Printing, 2020

# DEDICATIONS

*To GOD*

The day Your voice reached me; I understood my purpose.

*Cristian*

This book is dedicated to the one soul who gave me life the day he was born, my son, Cristian Andres Chavez. You are my grounding force and my North Star in this crazy journey of life. When the world came down on us hard, you gave me the strength to breathe, because I knew I was breathing for the both of us. You are and will always be the symbol of a fight worth fighting. You have filled my universe with a joy that can never be replicated. I am so incredibly proud of who you are and who you will ultimately become. As I see you launch into your own life, I stand on the sidelines, overjoyed at the man you are, knowing you will do so much good as you pursue your own purpose and legacy. I love you beyond measure and more than words can ever express.

## Lizet

Your friendship came at a time when God was creating a new mold of me. You showed me that accepting a simple hug can be life changing and as I lived through hardships, you assured me that everything was going to be okay, and you helped me believe it until it became a reality. When everyone else closed their doors on Cris, Mona and I, you opened yours and welcomed us into your home. We will always be grateful and cherish the memories made. And I cannot thank you enough for the life you have given to our dearest Mona-me.

## Maria Cristina

La paz, el amor, la comprensión y el cariño que nos brindaste a Cristian y a mi es algo que por siempre te agradeceré. Tu cariño, sabiduría, y creencia en mí han sido mi guia para sobrepasar mis dificultades. Mas aun por tu ayuda, empese este camino de ayudar a otros contando mi historia. Tu amistad ha sido un regalo inmenso del Universo! Te quiero mucho!

## My Siblings

Sergio, I am incredibly proud of the person you are. You have survived the unthinkable and shown that strength, determination, and love can come from the worst of experiences. You always have a special place in my heart, and I love you very much. To my other siblings: I wish each of you inner peace, reconciliation and prosperity in your respective lives.

## *Mis Padres*

Papi y Mami; por ustedes cuento mi historia y he entendido que hicieron lo mejor que pudieron hacer bajo las circunstancias. A pesar de todo lo que hemos pasado, les agradesco por darme mi vida y la oportunidad de ser alguien en este pais.

# A NOTE FROM THE AUTHOR

I used to believe I could not write this book until I became "successful." People who heard of my story always encouraged me to share it with the world, but I brushed off the suggestion for years because I was still fiercely working to get to that final destination called "success." Without reaching that arbitrary goal I believed I lacked credibility. But then I started to define what the word "success" really meant to me.

Would being a distinguished professional qualify me as successful? How about when I settled down inside that proverbial white-picket fence? Or was it something bigger? Maybe I would need to own a mansion, have a substantial bank account, and host lavish parties for celebrity friends to be considered a success.

In the end, I realized none of these things mattered and that my personal success happened the day I woke up knowing that I was living with complete awareness of simply being alive. I had fresh air to breathe, healthy feet to walk on, food to nourish my body, and a Universe that would provide for my needs–if I were brave enough to ask. No, success had nothing to do with material possessions or professional accolades. My own success had come from not only surviving my past, but from using everything I had learned along my difficult journey to help others. Although my life has not been easy and I have been knocked down many times, I found a way to get up, dust myself off, and keep moving forward. For far too long, I let my life's circumstances define me. I was unwanted. I was abused. I was a victim. I was an immigrant, and then, a deportee. Once I started to define "success" on my terms, I began the process of redefining myself.

My story is not easy to hear or read. I am opening the door to my turbulent past today with the hope that it will help you through your own struggles and to assure you that, just when you think you can't possibly survive your pain or circumstances... I am living proof that you absolutely can.

# CONTENTS

# | 1 |

# THE BROKEN CHILD

*"She was brave and strong and broken all at once."*

– ANNA FUNDER

———⟨⟩———

I looked over my shoulder one last time as I raced down the street as fast as my beaten-up sneakers could take me. The building I called home for the last three years grew smaller and less threatening in the distance. She was in the shower when I made my escape.

*Please, please don't let her see me.*

My heart pounded in my throat as I ran, and my backpack, stuffed with every piece of clothing I could cram in it, slapped against my back with every step. My head ached and the wounds on my scalp had started to bleed again. I was running for my life and this was my final dash to freedom. I was fourteen years old.

The previous night's beating had been the worst yet. I had made it into the house just seconds before my mother. When I burst through the front door, my dad was sitting at the dining room table enjoying a pink Hostess SnoBall and a tall glass of milk, blissfully unaware of the violent scene that had just unfolded between my mother and me. He tried to engage me in conversation, but I was too traumatized to speak. Unlike my dad, I knew all too well what was about to happen.

My mother was in a full-blown rage when she came through the door. Without saying a word, she charged past my dad and grabbed me by my hair. She dragged me through the kitchen toward the basement door, opened it, and flung me down the stairs. She then turned off the light and slammed the basement door shut.

My face hit the cold concrete floor as I landed hard at the bottom of the steps. I laid still for a moment before checking my arms and legs to make sure they weren't broken. I had some bumps and a rash of splinters from tumbling down the wooden stairs, but thankfully, no serious injuries. I sat in stillness and in the dark basement. On the other side of the door my mother was screaming. She told my dad that Jefferson High School had called to tell her I had been absent for four days and that I had been cutting classes regularly for a while. It was all true. I did cut school—more often lately, but I didn't realize I'd missed so many days in a row. I had lost count, and it was about to cost me bigtime.

My parents didn't allow me to hang out with my friends after school, so cutting class was the way I got time with them. Being with my friends gave me a safe space and allowed me to be myself. More importantly, it got me away from all the trouble at home. I joined my high school basketball team for the same reason—so I could be with friends outside of school hours and not be questioned about it. My plan was perfect, or so I thought. Admittedly, I sometimes ditched the games to do other things without my parents knowing.

That's what I had done that night, and my mother caught me. It was one of the last home games before winter break. I intended to go, but my friends and my then boyfriend were going to have some fun at an amusement park in a town about an hour away from home in Elizabeth, NJ, and I didn't want to miss out. I skipped school, and we spent the whole day driving with the windows down and the stereo blaring, hanging out at Six Flags Amusement Park. The plan was that my boyfriend would drop me off at school before the game ended, so I would be there when my mother came to pick me up. My parents would be furious if they found out I had lied and skipped the basketball game, but that wasn't the biggest issue I'd have to deal with. My boyfriend was almost twenty years old. My parents had forbidden me to see him, enraged at the thought of any man near me with romantic intentions.

We were having so much fun that evening that we lost track of time. We were running late. I was frantic as we barreled towards the school. Panic mounting, I prayed that we would get there before my mother. We had almost made it when we caught what felt like the longest red light in history while waiting to pull up into the school. I scanned the surrounding area for anyone who knew me–and who might be inclined to tell my parents that I wasn't at the game.

That's when I saw her.

My mother's little Toyota Corolla was parked in a shopping center across the street, directly facing us with the headlights off. And that's when she saw me. I gasped and my stomach lurched. Head spinning, I thought I might vomit. My mother's car roared to life on the opposite side of the intersection. My boyfriend followed my gaze and spotted the Corolla. The light turned green, but he was too stunned to move. "Drive! Drive! Drive!" I screamed as I punched his shoulder. "Drive now!"

He sped off, and for ten minutes we led my mother on a high-speed chase around Elizabeth, me screaming incoherently about how she would kill me and yelling at him to keep driving. When we finally lost her, my boyfriend pulled over and stopped on the side of the road. "I'm sorry, Erika," he said. "This has to stop." I now realize the trouble he could have faced had we been pulled over that night. He was legally an adult and I was a minor, and with the way he was driving, he could have been arrested for some serious criminal charges. But that's not what I was thinking about then. My fight or flight instinct had kicked in, and I was just trying to survive. Within seconds, my mother had caught up to our car and was at the side of the door, reaching through the open passenger-side window. She grabbed a handful of my hair and pulled me out through the window. I fell onto the sidewalk and she continued shaking me around by my hair as she screamed, *"Berraca Trafuga! Me las vas a pagar!"* - *Freaking Thief! You are going to pay!* My mother was a tiny woman, only four-foot-nine, but she was strong. And when she was angry, it was as if she had super-human strength. Not letting go of my hair, she dragged me down the sidewalk to the Corolla and shoved me into the back seat, using the door to cram me inside. As she sped off, I caught a glimpse of my boyfriend. He was sitting inside of his car, mouth hanging open in shock as he watched us drive away.

The drive home seemed to unfold in slow motion, even though my mother was driving well over the speed limit. I still don't know how she managed to shift gears on her manual-transmission Toyota while throwing punches at me in the back seat. She finally made a right turn onto our dead-end street and stopped to parallel park the car in front of our building. Taking advantage of the opportunity to get into our apartment a few steps ahead of her, I threw open the door and bolted.

Back in the dark basement amidst the piles of rotting garbage, dirty laundry, and unused gardening tools, I could hear my mother continuing to scream upstairs. My dad was mostly silent while she railed on about me skipping school, but as soon as she mentioned the boyfriend, the basement lights flicked on, the door flew open, and the two of them charged down the stairs. My dad got to me first.

He grabbed me by my arms, pulled me to my feet, and shoved me into the middle of the basement where he forced me to my knees to beg for forgiveness. He was screaming right in my ear, but I couldn't hear anything he was saying. I was focused on my mother, who seemed to be looking for something. When she finally found the industrial broom resting against the wall in the corner of the basement, my heart sank. My stomach lurched again. My mother grabbed the handle of the heavy-duty broom with both hands, raised it above her head, and delivered the first blow. She continued hitting me with the wooden broom stick for what seemed like an eternity, while my dad held me in place by my shoulders. There are no words that can accurately describe my mother's rage that night. "Blind rage" comes close but still does not capture what happened in that base-ment. Blow after blow after blow to my head and body. Her anger was all-consuming. The pain was so intense that I went numb at some point during the beating. I don't remember whether I cried or begged her to stop or tried to shield myself, but I do remember what she said as she beat me. Two phrases delivered between blows.

*"You will never amount to anything!"*

*"You are the worst thing that has ever come out of me!"*

At one point, my two little brothers and my sister gathered at the top of the basement steps to see what was going on. When they saw the violent scene below, they began crying and begging my parents to stop. I screamed for my sister to call the police, but as she turned to walk back up the stairs, my parents threatened to beat her next if she did. My sister and brothers were ordered to go back upstairs and shut the door behind them. The beating finally ended when my dad saw the blood dripping down my face. It was as if the sight of my blood snapped him back to reality. He let go of my shoulders, grabbed my mother, and pushed her backwards away from me. He ordered me to go upstairs to clean myself up then created a human barricade between me and my mother so I could pass her.

I ran into the bedroom where my sister, mother, and one of my brothers slept every night in a full-sized bed and slammed the door behind me. My dad came into the bedroom a few minutes later. He was still seething with anger. He poked me hard in the shoulder with his index finger while screaming in my face–so close that I could feel his spit spraying my skin. *"Haceme el favor y te me compones. Deja de llorar!"* He yelled at me in Spanish saying to compose myself and stop crying. Then suddenly, he stopped yelling and told me to get up. I felt a chill run down my spine. *"Cojé el abrigo y metete al carro,"* Get your coat on and get in the car, he instructed. *"No has terminado con tu castigo!'* You're not done with your punishment.

I stared out the window of our rusty four-door Oldsmobile Cutlass Supreme as my dad drove towards U.S. Route 1/9 that led from Elizabeth to New Brunswick, where he worked at a factory, handcutting rubber templates used to create images for boxed-food packaging. I knew the route well. Sometimes, when I had a day off from school, I went to work with him, and he would describe step-by-step how he did his job. I was always so impressed and wanted to be just like him. On the way to the factory, we would stop at a little mom-and-pop coffee shop a few blocks away from the highway where my dad always ordered a *café con leche* and a toasted bun with butter for breakfast and a ham-and-cheese sandwich to go. I was closer with my dad than my siblings were, and this was a routine that only we shared. Even though I always wished that he would stop my mother when she was out of control, I loved my dad and cherished the time we spent at the factory together. The coffee shop was a bonus, one I always looked forward to. But when my dad pulled up to the shop that night and parked his car, it was the last place I wanted to be.

Over the years my dad had become friendly with the owner, a fellow Colombian. I had asked my dad to speak to him about hiring me as a part-time cashier so I could start earning my own money.

My dad had approached him with the proposal just a few weeks earlier and the owner agreed. All I had to do was go in and ask for the job.

*"Salite!"* Get out! my dad said, shutting the ignition. *"Anda y pregunta por trabajo. Si queres mandarte sola, entonces vas a conseguir trabajo!"* Go ask for a job. If you want to make your own decisions, then you can start by getting a job.

I had been planning on going to the shop the following day, but my dad was intent on teaching me a lesson that night. So, there I was, at closing time on a Friday night, my face swollen and caked in drying blood, about to have my first job interview. I got out of the car and slowly approached the front door to the shop. When I stepped inside, the owner was standing behind the register reading the newspaper. I can't imagine what must have gone through his mind when he looked up and saw me standing there, bloodied and crying. His body stiffened. He removed his glasses, then asked me what had happened.

"I'm sorry," I stammered. "I ju-just want to know if I can have the cashier job." Again, he demanded I tell him what happened. And again, I responded. "Ca-can you please let me have the cashier job?" We went back and forth like this a few times before he walked around the counter towards me and told me to leave. "No, please," I begged. "You don't understand. Can you just let me know if I can have the job?" By now he was angry and threatened to call the police if I didn't leave immediately. "Yes!" I cried. "Please! Call the police!" He then grabbed me by the arm, shoved me out the door, and locked it behind me. I stood there for a moment, humiliated, and defeated, but that was the whole point of the lesson I was being taught. I wanted to collapse in a heap right there on the sidewalk, but my dad honked the horn and waved for me to get in the car.

*"Y?"* So? he asked as I slid into the passenger seat. *"No me dio el trabajo."* I didn't get the job, I said quietly, staring down at the floor. My dad turned the key in the ignition and the Oldsmobile's engine

groaned. *"Claro que no. No te lo mereces."* Of course, you didn't, he said... You don't deserve it.

Words have tremendous power. The beating that night was terrifying, but my parents' words had the greatest impact on me. My mother, lost in rage, had told me I was the worst thing that ever came out of her and that I would never amount to anything in life. Those words broke the child in me. They also shaped my life from that night forward fueling my drive, my passion, my purpose and empowering me as a woman. That night I made a conscious decision to prove her wrong, but I knew I couldn't fulfill this mission as long as I lived under my parents' roof. The following morning, I stuffed my backpack with clothes and left our family home for the last time.

The run to my destination, Hogar Nazareth, a women's shelter run by the Congregation of Siervas de San Jose, felt like it took forever even though it was less than a mile away. When I finally arrived at the side entrance, I was out of breath and my legs felt like they would give out from under me. I knocked on the door and did my best to stifle the fear rising inside me. Sister Filomena opened the door, took one look, and without saying a word, hugged me and brought me inside. I had found my new home.

At 14 years old around the time I left my home

Elizabeth High School Girl's Basketball Team

# | 2 |

# HOSTAGE TO HOARDING

*"Hoarding is the persistent difficulty discarding or parting with possessions because of a perceived need to save them."*

– MAYO CLINIC

---

For as far back as I could remember, everywhere we lived, we lived as hoarders. I was completely oblivious that this was not normal until about age nine or ten when I went over my friend Valorie's house for the first time and noticed that her house was super clean and everything was organized in its place. My parents would occasionally let me go over to her house down the street to have a play date but whenever she came over to play at my house, she wasn't allowed to go inside. She would bring her toys and dolls over and we would only be allowed to play on my front steps. I would refrain from offering her anything to drink from inside of my house because if she ever needed to use the bathroom, she wouldn't be allowed to come inside. In the event she would ever ask to use the bathroom, she and I would walk to a restaurant about a block away so she can use the restroom there and come back to continue playing. I'm sure Valorie knew something wasn't right but she spared me with the mortifying embarrassment of asking and just went with it.

Our apartment was always a fetid disaster. Dirty dishes piled on the center table in the living room evidenced dinners past. Stacks of newspapers and junk mail stolen from the neighbors' mailboxes filled two corners of the living room. A mountain of unfolded clothes was piled high in another corner. Rumpled bedsheets and pillows on the sofas revealed where my brother slept every night. In the kitchen, garbage cluttered the surface of the cabinet countertops and every possible inch of space was covered. Unpleasant odors leaked from empty milk gallons encircled with yellow crusts. The mingling stench of empty cans of black beans, the contents of which were dumped on our dinner plates whenever my mother felt like cooking would permeate the air. Added to that were a variety of empty cereal boxes, months' worth of soiled paper towels, dirty frying pans, and a sink overflowing with dishes that had not been washed in weeks. Bedrooms were filled to the ceiling with broken furniture and trash bags full of dirty old clothes and garbage. Closet doors were pinned opened against the walls with mounds of broken items and clothes spilling out of them. And the carpet had never seen a vacuum cleaner in its lifespan.

For normal families, a dining room table is a place for family gatherings, to share blessed meals and conversations. Ours was not. Our dining table was the mecca for garbage collection. I couldn't tell you what color or material our table was made of. During elementary school, I would wake up late for school almost every morning. The Spanish Radio station, Radio WADO would be blasting in the background, competing with my mother's screaming that we would all be late, and it would be our own fault. She would rip into my hair with a wire brush, yanking my head from side to side as she yelled to drive home her point. I endured the hair pulling quietly as I knew better than to complain or she would use the brush to hit me on the head and "give me something to really cry about." After my hair was pulled into a too-tight ponytail, I carefully used my forearm to push back six inches of garbage from the edge of the table to make room for my breakfast of champions–a mug of Swiss Miss hot chocolate with marshmallows and a plate of crackers with mayonnaise. Then there would be a shoving and yelling fest to the car as I held my tears back and threw myself into the back seat of the Corolla. I would have a death grip on the door handle as she raced like Speedy Gonzalez to the school which was only six blocks away. By the time I sat at my desk in class I was a nervous, sleepy, wreck of a fourth grader.

My parents argued profusely about our living conditions but nothing ever changed. My mother would give us dirty, wet clothes with holes in them to go to school. My little brother once went to class holding his pants up the entire day because it was missing the button and the zipper. She sent him to school demanding he hold his pants up and he better not complain about it. She would pat talcum powder on my dad's dirty and smelly socks as she threw them at him to use for work in the mornings. She would beat us if we tried to use the washer machine ourselves and would incite my dad to a fist fight if he tried to do it as well. He never did. My dad would try profusely to convince my mother that we could live in a clean normal home if she would just allow us to throw away the garbage but she would adamantly refuse and would threaten to become violent if we tried to do something about it. We were hostages of my mother's hoarding disorder for years until one night when we saw an opportunity.

We had just returned from a summer vacation in Colombia. My dad worked overtime nights and weekends to save money so he could afford buying airline tickets for us to visit my mother's family in Colombia for the summer. We would only go every two or three years because it took him that long to save for five roundtrip tickets for my mother, my siblings and me. My dad was never able to go because he had to stay and work for our family. That year when we arrived back home to the States, my mother had to be taken to the emergency room for appendicitis. She was immediately admitted for surgery. Being home without my mother for the first time sparked an idea between my dad and one of my mother's brothers who was visiting from Colombia. They decided we would surprise her and clean out THE ENTIRE APARTMENT. We figured her hoarding was because the years of accumulation of trash had just reached an overwhelming level. We thought a fresh, new start would make all the difference.

My dad purchased new silverware, dishware, cleaning supplies, furniture, and more. You name it, he bought it! We were ecstatic and worked tirelessly for hours, removing every piece of garbage from the house and cleaning like it had never been cleaned before. When we were done, the garbage pile on the curb outside was five feet tall and fifteen feet wide. It was embarrassing to see our neighbors as they looked on, confused about where all the trash came from. We had lived in that pile of garbage for years. Walking back into the house after our massive purge brought us to tears. A beige dining table greeted us with a vase of fresh flowers in its center. The kitchen counters were completely clean and unobstructed. The bedrooms were organized and peaceful. My siblings and I hugged each other ecstatic with a pure sense of accomplishment–welcoming our new reality. No more chaos. No more fights. No more garbage. And no more mice and roaches crawling throughout our home.

When the garbage truck arrived to pick up Mount Trashmore, it was as if the entire weight of that trash pile lifted off our shoulders and we could finally breathe in relief. A few days later, my mother was due to come home and we were beyond eager for the reveal. Still, as excited as we were, there was a shadow of fear that she may not be as happy as we were with this extreme home makeover. Boy, did we underestimate that feeling.

When my mother was released from the hospital, she was told to take it easy, get some rest, and slowly get back into her routine.

However, when she walked in and caught the first glimpse of what we had done to the apartment, she went ballistic. She was screaming profanities and pacing the house like a crazed lunatic. She cursed us out and kicked my visiting uncle out of the house. Her angry tirade went on for hours. That night, after we had all gone to bed, she limped out into the neighborhood, still weak from her surgery and started rummaging through our neighbor's garbage. She picked up every piece of garbage she could find and began placing it all over our home. Within a week, the apartment looked like it had never been touched before and our new dining table had gone into hiding, just like the old one. In very short order, we officially became hoarders again.

My mother suffers from a severe hoarding disorder. She was never diagnosed because she never admitted to having a problem and refused any treatment. We lived with her disorder until each one of my siblings moved out one by one. My dad, after twenty six years of marriage and fighting with her every day of those twenty six years, was kicked out of the house by her who told him never to come home again. A couple of years later, they were officially divorced. Today, she lives alone with her disorder.

Second Grade

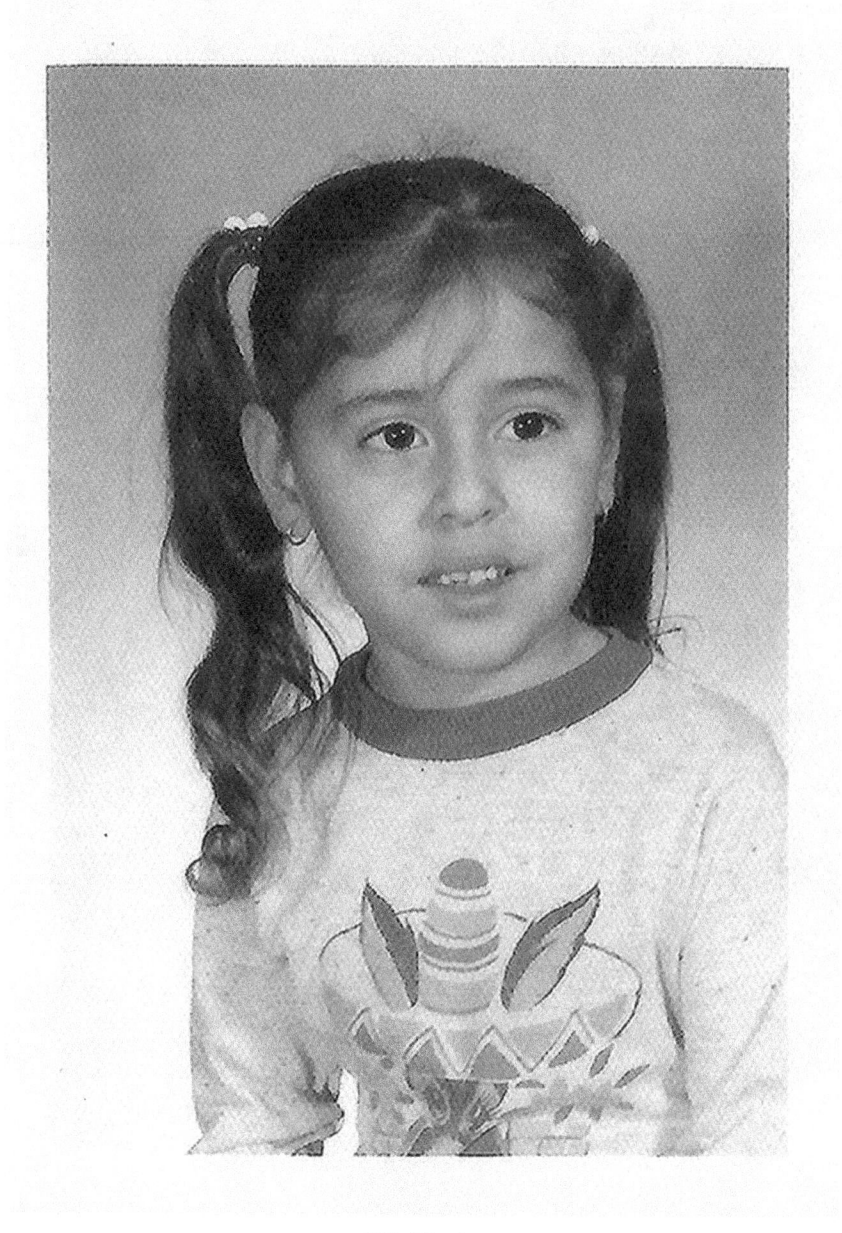

Third Grade

# | 3 |

# NEW BEGINNINGS

*"The first step towards getting somewhere is to decide you're not going to stay where you are."*

– J. P. MORGAN

———⟨∘⟩———

Hogar Nazareth, was a two story building located on the corner of East Jersey Street and Smith Street next door to a convent. It was a safe haven for local kids run by the Nuns from the convent that serviced Saint Michael's, Saint Anthony's, and St. Joseph's churches. The first floor was an after-school hall that was open to underprivileged kids from the neighborhood in an effort to keep them safe and off the streets. The Nuns provided a space where the kids could do homework, have snacks, interact with one another and where they could be mentored and tutored by the Nuns. The second floor had been converted into a five-bedroom apartment that offered room rentals for women who were displaced, had no family, or who were struggling to get back on their feet and couldn't afford standard rent. The upstairs unit was run by a Spanish Nun named Sister Filomena.

I had learned about Hogar Nazareth earlier in my life when I befriended a girl named Maria who was studying to be a Nun and attended services at Saint Anthony's. I met Maria during catechism class as she was one of the volunteers that helped out on Sundays. She was always so nice to the class and smart and she'd give us great advice on anything we wanted to talk about. Shortly after meeting her, I began confiding my family's abuse to her in search of guidance on how to handle it. Out of concern, she would continuously beg me to report this to the authorities, but I always refused out of fear of what would happen to me or even my parents. One day, she told me about Hogar Nazareth and asked me to consider that as my safe place to go to if the situation ever became unbearable at home. Although the apartment was not meant to house minors, she felt it necessary to offer this option to me due to my circumstances. She had shared my situation with the Nuns and asked if they would consider making an exception for me. Eventually, the Nuns agreed and said that if I ever knocked on their door, they would let me in.

When I ran away from home and my mother realized I had escaped the prison of my bedroom, I'm sure she panicked. It was the first time I had run away and back then there were no cell phones or Find My iPhone apps to track people's whereabouts. She didn't have my friends' numbers or any way to check my last text messages. I could have been anywhere and she would have no way of finding me. I had anticipated that one day I would run away to Nazareth. I put a plan in place with a friend and she knew that if she received my call, she was to drive to my parent's house, ask to speak only with my dad and let him know where I was. She also knew not to tell my mother where I was.

The day I arrived at the Nun's house, Sister Filomena brought me upstairs and sat with me at the dining room table and offered me tea. For a few hours, we sat as I recounted everything that happened to me. I explained why I couldn't go back to my mother's house and I pled with anguish as I asked if I could live with them. Even though I could see the empathy in her eyes, she explained that because I was a minor, they legally could not keep me there or let me stay. She explained that I would need to have consent from at least one parent to be able to live there temporarily. I knew that my dad would soon find my whereabouts if everything would go as I planned. And I knew that I would have one chance at stating my case with him to have him sign me off to the Nun's care.

That evening, there was a knock at the door of the Nun's house, and I knew it would be my dad. I remember sitting at the entrance table with him and Sister Filomena going over what had happened the night before. My dad made sure he left out certain details that would paint him in a bad light and instead he profusely apologized for my mother's loss of temper. With Sister Filomena by my side, I said I was never going back to the house. I knew my mother would kill me if she ever got her hands on me again. I had defied and insulted her in the worst way possible by running away. She also knew that this meant I would have told someone what she had done to me so I would surely pay the price for that. Knowing my dad wouldn't stop her from retaliating against me, I asked him to sign a consent for me to live at the Nun's house. We spent hours arguing back and forth as he insisted that I needed to be with my own family, that leaving the house to live somewhere else was not going to fix any problems. I cried for him to understand the severity of what had happened and that it would only get worst. I begged him to snap out of his unrealistic expectations of what our family was supposed to be and to give me a chance at a new beginning. Sister Filomena periodically chimed in and tried to reason with my dad by recapping the facts of what we told her had happened the previous night and the detrimental effect it would continue to have on me.

After hours of crying, talking, and negotiating, he gave in. My dad signed the release that would allow me to live there indefinitely. From that point on, I theoretically still belonged to my parents but the Nuns now had parental consent to house a minor under their care. Sister Filomena then proceeded to go over the expectations of the house both with my dad as well as with me. The rules of the house were simple: for me, I was expected to contribute to the keeping of the house, show respect to all the women that lived there and abide by the curfews in place. All were expected to get along and chip in with the cleaning and cooking duties and also spending time together as a family. For my dad, she let him know that the women who lived there paid their share of the rent. Because she understood this was a unique situation, she told my dad that he could pay $100 a month to cover my food expenses. My dad and I sat there nodding quietly as Sister Filomena proceeded to inform us of my new life. Once she was done, she looked at us both making sure we understood. I eagerly shook my head yes and then looked at my dad. My dad sulked in silence for a few minutes lost in his struggle. I know he wanted me to go back home because in his mind, whether it was good or bad, he always fought for us to stay together as a family. And to some degree I am sure he had contemplated leaving my mother and the kids many times before himself. But year after year he stayed holding on to the slim chance and hope that one day my mother would come to her senses and not only accept she had a problem but also do something about it. But she never did. When he realized that signing me over was the right thing to do, he arose in defeat from the chair, shook Sister Filomena's hand, turned to me, and patted the top of my head as he walked towards the door. I stood there watching him and even though I had an urge to run and hug him tight grateful for what he had just done, I chose instead to nestle my shaking body in Sister Filomena's cradling embrace as my eyes clouded with tears.

My dad didn't look back. Without a word, he walked out the door and slammed it shut behind him. I stood there thinking, *Wow... if only you had just stood up for what was right even if it was against my mother... I wouldn't be here to begin with.* But I have learned throughout the years that everything happens for a reason and what he did that night for me, changed my life forever.

**Sister Filomena shoveling snow in front of Hogar Nazareth**

With Sister Filomena & Maria who introduced me to Hogar Nazareth

Cleaning snow with Maria and one of my roommates, Loli

# | 4 |

# LIVING AT THE NUN'S HOUSE

*"You can't be brave if you've only had wonderful things happen to you."*

– MARY TYLER MOORE

———— ⟡ ————

The first night at The Nun's House, I showered in a clean tub and used a clean towel with fragrant toiletries included in my welcoming kit. As I dried my battered and swollen face, I stared at my reflection in the mirror and relived the night before. Images flashed through my mind as I examined the person staring back from the mirror in front of me. Here I was now, showered and bruised, but sensing there was hope for me yet. That night I slept in a warm, clean bed that felt like absolute heaven. There was no yelling and no fighting. The bedsheets smelled of vanilla. The girl who would be my new roommate was out for the weekend. That night was the first night I learned what it was to feel at peace.

When I woke up to a knock on my bedroom door that following morning, I was greeted with the warm smile and the soft-spoken blessing of Sister Filomena. I knew I was embarking on a new chapter in my life. When I think about when I began to build the framework that helped me structure the life I have now, it always leads back to the Nuns' House. I have so many wonderful memories of sitting together at dinners talking about our days. My roommates were women from all over the world, Michelle was from Argentina, America was from El Salvador, Stephany was Puerto Rican, Loli was Ecuadorian and Sister Filomena was from Spain. Naturally, our home-cooked meals were good enough to put any local restaurant out of business with this array of cuisines. To this day, I still cook a meal I learned from Michelle which she called the Argentinian Shepherd's Pie, which funny enough is the typical American Shepherd's Pie with her Latin twist. At night, we would play board games and Truth or Dare. We were required to meet as a family in the living room to spend time together and learn from one another. This is a practice that is missing in our culture today, but it is one of the most important values I learned. The two years I lived at the Nuns' House laid the groundwork for the way I live my life. I had my first taste of family unity and togetherness there. I learned how to keep a home, how to nourish a family, and how to plant seeds of kindness and compassion. I learned of integrity, love, and friendship. But familial experiences were not everything I learned. Being around the Nuns made me increasingly curious to learn a different view of the Catholic religion than what I had been exposed to when I was younger.

As I established my new life at the Nun's House, I also adopted new routines that they had in place. One of them was attending Sunday service every week. I spent most of my time transfixed as I gazed at the crowds of people, every Sunday, reciting the priests' chants. It was mesmerizing to watch everyone pour themselves in unison at the direction of one maestro. I also noticed as the altar boys, doting their white robes, would carefully choose the offerings they would carry to the altar at the start of each service. They looked so proud to lead the priest at the head of the procession it made you want to be part of something that regal. Week after week, I would watch how they would be so precise with their movements and wait for cues to walk up to the alter and deliver the items to the priest. They invoked respect and honor and I wanted to be a part of it. One day I went back home with the Nuns and said... "I want to be an Alter Girl!"

My excitement quickly faded as I was told that the church did not allow girls or women to be part of the Altar team. When I asked the sisters why girls could not participate, the only answer anyone had was, "It just hasn't been done." To me, this was an invitation to build my case. I wrote a letter to the Church– one to the priest and one to the archdiocese. I asked why my gender prevented me from performing the same services as the altar boys did. After all, I told them, I was just as capable of walking down the aisle and assisting a priest during Mass. I demanded answers and when I did not get responses, I sent my inquiries again and again. After countless letters and requests, I finally received a letter from the Archdiocese acknowledging my countless letters. It stated that after thorough consideration, they agreed that there was no reason that I could not perform the same service as altar boys and so... I became an altar girl. There is something to be said for persistence and not accepting a simple no for an answer. Learned that early on!

I was so proud that first Sunday as I put the white robe over my clothes, picked up the offerings I was responsible for taking to the altar, and led the priest in for the service. Accomplishing something so huge was beyond anything I had ever experienced. It was an immense win for me even though I faced harsh criticism from the congregation for changing a tradition as old as the church itself.

The nuns back at the house were not thrilled with me either but they were proud of my determination and persistence. The day my letter from the archdiocese arrived, I ran into the house yelling and waving the letter in the air. Sister Filomena held me in her arms and told me how proud she of me for accomplishing something that I had worked so hard for. Although she was not completely comfortable with the church's new progressive stance, she was wise and loving enough to not let her beliefs diminish my joy. Instead, she rejoiced with me and supported me for standing up for what I believed and for fighting for it. It was the first time in my life that anyone had told me they were proud of me. Those words sank deep into my soul as my body sank deep into her warm embrace and in that moment, I realized I was worth fighting for, and I had a voice that mattered.

The year that followed, I began to fix all the things that were broken inside of me. In that period, I began to lay a solid foundation for my future with the help of Sister Filomena. If you can imagine what the "perfect grandma" looks like, that was Sister Filomena. She had soft white hair that peeked out from under her nun's habit and deep smile lines around her eyes and mouth. She was from Spain and spoke with a heavy Castilian accent which made every sentence sound like a song. She was quick to offer a tight embrace whether you needed it or not. Her rose-scented lotion lingered on your clothing for hours after those hugs. Sister Filomena knew from the beginning that I would not be an easy task, but she accepted the challenge with grace and wisdom.

The Nun's House had family rules like the ones you would have in a normal home. Our rooms had to be spotless. We had to make our beds in the morning, and the nuns were known to do random spot checks. Closing our bedroom doors was frowned upon. We were a family and a closed door meant you weren't communicating and connecting with others. These rules helped the girls living in the home bond as sisters. The apartment on the second floor overlooked one of the town's busiest street corners. The entrance to the apartment was located on the side of the building past a black, wrought-iron gate and up a steep set of stairs. Immediately beyond the front door was a foyer. Men were not allowed in the interior living quarters, so this was where we met with visiting family or dates. Inside was a large kitchen/dining room combo, a family room, five bedrooms, and a single bathroom for the apartment's ten residents. Sister Filomena had her own bedroom. Each of the other guest rooms had two twin-size beds, a matching nightstand, a large shared closet, and room for a small dresser.

My room was in the back of the apartment, overlooking East Jersey Street. From my window I could see the local bodega. The police were there often to handle one problem or another. At night, vagabonds would hang out playing loud music and whistling at passersby. It wasn't safe to walk around the neighborhood after dark, but I never felt more at peace in my life. I had a clean room decorated to showcase my flourishing personality. I had the love and warmth of a new makeshift family. It could not have felt more like home. It is said that we are all products of our environment, that the tools we need to navigate life are handed down from generation to generation. In my case, I was given a toolbox filled with broken tools, the same set of tools my parents had been given. The only thing I could have possibly built with those tools was a future filled with the same pain, misery, and dysfunction that I had grown up with. At the age of fourteen, I made a conscious decision to end the cycle and get myself a new toolbox. We may not all be given the right tools in life, but we all have a choice whether to use them or not. I exercised mine.

Everything I had endured up until that moment led me to that place. The night of the beating was the catalyst, but the groundwork had been laid long before. The only way to fully understand what led to my desperate act that night is to go back to the very beginning of my story.

My first birthday at the Nun's house was very emotional

The Sisters & roommates gave me a surprise party to cheer me up

# | 5 |

# AN AMERICAN DREAM

*"We may come from different places and have different stories, but
we share common hopes and one very American Dream"*

**– BARACK H. OBAMA II**

———⟨❧⟩———

My parents lived across the street from each other in a small bar-
rio in Medellin, Colombia, where everyone knew everyone. My dad
says he fell in love with my mother the moment he laid eyes on
her. That doesn't surprise me. My mother, though a simple woman,
was thin and elegant with poise and a strong presence. Whenever
he talked about that time in his life, his eyes would light up and he
would relive those feelings of true love all over again. The way my
dad loved my mother was both profound and sick. It often blinded
him to reasoning and logic but there was no doubt in my mind that
he was head over heels for her.

My mother was the oldest of sixteen children (only twelve of whom made it to adulthood). She was pulled out of school around third grade so she could help raise her younger siblings as my grandparents continued to procreate. Just a child herself, she was expected to take care of the younger children and manage the household chores, which included hand-washing clothes, then ironing them, preparing three full meals a day, and keeping a pristine home for the family that continued to grow. She pretty much raised children long before she had her own.

My dad, the third child of seven, had an even tougher childhood. His father was a militant beast who scarred my dad for life. My dad shared stories with us about what it was like for him growing up. He told us that his dad would come home after coddling his mistress all day and he would forbid his wife to feed or care for my dad or the other children. He ordered my grandmother to lock him out of the home for days. Terrified of this vicious, abusive monster she married, my grandmother obeyed. My dad was six years old. He told us that he would walk to local bus stations and barter with the drivers. If they would allow him to sleep inside the buses overnight, he would wake up before dawn and clean the buses before they began their routes. He was an entrepreneur before he was old enough to spell the word much less know what it meant. In his young dismal life, my dad begged for food and compassion from strangers. He often walked the streets barefoot, hungry, and aimless. As he got older, he found solace and refuge in the home of one of his aunts– Rosita – who took him in as one of her own and gave him the maternal nurturing and love he so desperately needed. She made him feel worthy and gave him the greatest gift of all, spiritual wealth. But by the time he found her, his innocence was already damaged.

My dad courted my mother for a few years before he finally proposed. Neither family approved of their relationship so when he proposed, things only became harder. According to relatives, a few days before their wedding day, my mother decided to cancel the wedding. My dad was so heartbroken and distraught that he fell violently ill and couldn't get out of bed. Even though she was unhappy about the wedding, my paternal grandmother was so worried about my dad that she walked to my mother's house and begged her to reconsider the marriage. My mother eventually conceded. On June 9, 1972, the day after my dad's twenty-third birthday, they were pronounced husband and wife. I arrived on August 1, 1975. Less than two years later, my sister was born. From the beginning my parents struggled to make ends meet. My Abuelita Rosa, my mother's mom, took our family into her house so we can live with her. My mother stayed home to take care of us, and my dad spent most of the day desperately looking for employment. My parents would hear stories from my grandmother about how well my aunt and uncle (my mother's brother and my dad's sister, who married each other) were doing since they emigrated to New Jersey. My parents decided that they too wanted a shot at the American Dream.

It would not be an easy trip with two young daughters in tow. Traveling through Panama and Mexico was too dangerous. Instead, they decided to travel across South America flight hopping until we arrived at our destination. First flight was from Medellin to Cali, Colombia. Then from Cali to Quito and then to Guayaquil, Ecuador. From Ecuador to Nassau, Bahamas. From Nassau to Freeport. And finally, our last flight was from Freeport to Bimini. Our flight arrived safely to Bimini but unfortunately, my family had not made arrangements for a place to stay once we arrived. In somewhat of a panic, my dad started walking down the beaches and boat docks of the island while we spent the day at the beach. My dad came across two fishermen–a Cuban and an American– and managed to convince them to help us cross the Atlantic in their rickety fishing boats for four-thousand dollars. My dad shook hands with both men, paid the fee and later that night we all piled into the boat and set sail for our new home.

Over the years, I have thought about the fear and anxiety but also about the courage my parents must have had to take that trip. They knew there was no guarantee that we would make it to Miami. And even worst, there was no guarantee these fishermen would honor their hand-shake agreement and deliver us to our destination. They could have stolen the money and thrown us overboard at sea. While I don't remember a lot of that journey, my dad told us that the boats that crossed us through the Atlantic were barely seaworthy. Water seeped into the boat as we traveled across the sea and we were forced to hide in the cramped cabin below deck whenever the fisherman saw the Coast Guard in the distance. My dad recalls huddling us into him as he prayed that God would see us through. All the while feeling the water swishing at his feet while the fisherman sped through the moonlit waves. At one point, the water inside the cabin rose so high my dad thought we weren't going to survive the trip. But after hours at sea wondering whether we were going to make it alive, our vessel reached the Florida shore shortly before midnight. Early the next morning, we boarded a one-way Eastern Airlines flight to Newark, New Jersey where we would start our new life. We were filled with hope for the future but none of us could have imagined how quickly our dreams would fade and how short our time would be in our adopted homeland.

It is interesting how certain memories make an indelible impression while others do not. I have few memories of crossing the Atlantic in the Cuban fisherman's boat yet there are smaller details of my life in Elizabeth, New Jersey, that are etched on my brain forever. I remember our first home. It was on the first floor of 1421 Lexington Avenue in Elizabeth. The family that owned it was a couple named *Doña Malely* and *Don Barreto* who had two sons, Barney and Bryon. They were my first friends in America. I remember my sister's circus-themed birthday party, and I remember the old man who used to knock on our door from time to time offering to do mini photoshoots of us on his pet pony. For a small fee, of course. These were the good memories. We had food to eat and clothes on our backs, but the American Dream was not turning out the way my parents had imagined or hoped. My dad took on odds-and-ends jobs while my mother stayed home with the children, which eventually included my two younger brothers. Now a family of six, every penny my dad made went towards paying the bills and feeding us. There was never anything left over for the little things that bring big joy to a child's life. Perhaps that is why I've never forgotten the two-hour shopping extravaganza my uncle took my sister and me on and the terrible way the joy of that day was ripped away.

A few weeks after living in New Jersey, my uncle who had been living in the U.S. showed up one day at our house and announced that he would take my sister and I on a toy shopping spree. He had escorted us to his car and off we went to a popular toy store on Elizabeth Avenue & Broad Street. We arrived at the store shortly before they closed and as we made our way in the store my uncle said to us, "You can have whatever you can fit in a shopping cart," pointing to two carts. We were nervous and apprehensive. Could this really be happening? My sister and I were so small we could barely see above the handles of our shopping carts. At first, we walked slowly down each aisle, gently placing just a couple of items in our buggies, still in total disbelief that this was really happening. But our uncle challenged us insisting we load up with whatever we wanted and to hurry because they would soon be closing the store. Before long we had carts full of baby dolls with strollers, building blocks, Barbie's, G.I. Joe action figures, and anything else we could reach on the shelves. We giggled all the way home squished between overflowing bags of toys in the back seat of my uncle's Toyota Corolla.

We arrived home past our bedtime. My mother immediately intercepted the bags filled with toys, threw them in the back room of our apartment, and shut the door. That room was a hot spot for my mother's hoarding. It was filled with piles of clothing, garbage, and other assorted things she had "collected." We were told that when we behaved and if we did well in school, we would get to play with those toys. That never happened.

I was afraid of that room but I longed for the toys that I knew were just beyond the closed door. One afternoon while my mother was feeding one of my little brothers, desire trumping my fear, I quietly opened the door and stepped inside. The room was dark with only a sliver of light peeking through the blinds. I found the bag closest to the door, shoved my little hand in and pulled out a squeeze toy named Panic Pete. He was half the size of a Barbie doll and when you squeezed him, his blue eyes popped out and red knobs popped out of his ears. With my heart racing, I hid Pete inside my shirt and ran out of the room. I knew getting caught with that doll would earn me a beating so I hid him between my mattress and box spring and never told a soul what I had done. Every time I was able to go outside alone I brought Pete with me. Panic Pete was my prized possession.

By the time I was eight years old, we were living in a two-bedroom apartment on Third Avenue in Peterstown. It was dark with wood-paneled walls in the living area and was barely furnished, except for a single patio chair that my parents had dragged in from the neighbor's bulk-garbage pile. At night we could hear scratching from behind the paneled walls. Even at the age of eight, I knew that meant there was something living in there. At times I would hear my mother crying softly in her bed while I played in the other room. I didn't understand it then. My mother was the kind of woman who rarely expressed emotions other than anger and frustration. Looking back at her now as an adult, I have a deeper sense of empathy. She had left everything and everyone she knew to come to a new country for the promise of a better life for her family. I don't know if she ever had any dreams or ambitions for herself, but those were long gone as she spent her time alone all day responsible for four young children. My dad's extent of parenting was limited to providing us with a roof over our heads and food on our table. He spent a lot of evenings going to the local bars after work mostly on the weekends and would come home inebriated. Maybe it was his way of checking out of his reality. Or maybe this was his way of avoiding the constant fighting at home over the same problems of my mother's hoarding. My dad's drinking became his pacifier and gave my mother reason to justify her constant arguing. Life was hard to say the least, and it was about to get even harder.

Our time on Third Avenue would soon be cut short. In 1984 I was a third grader at Christopher Columbus School 15. One day my dad was detained by U.S. Immigration Authorities at the factory where he'd been working. It was a routine documentation check, but of course, my dad did not have papers to be in the United States legally. He was taken straight to the Immigration offices, and not long after authorities were at our door to collect the rest of us. What happened next is a blur. I was not old enough at the time to understand what was going on. I didn't know what the phrase "being deported" meant. I didn't know why officers were taking us from our home to the airport. My parents tried to hide their emotions but I knew something was terribly wrong. Our life in New Jersey was far from perfect but it was all I knew. And now we were being told we didn't belong in this country and couldn't stay here. Because my two younger brothers were American-born, my parents decided it was best to leave them in the United States under the care of friends. However, my parents, sister, and I were returned to Colombia. I don't recall the actual flight back to Colombia, but I remember walking into my grandmother's house and being greeted with both tears of sadness and warm embraces from my grandmother. I wasn't sure if she was happy to see us or sad that we had returned.

The Jacqueline Kennedy School was down the block from my grandmother's house in Belen, Medellin. As new residents, my parents enrolled me for school, and I was to start my new third grade there. As my parents walked me and my sister to school on our first day, we were briefed on what could be said at the new school and what was to be kept "in the family." Gossip was the neighborhood's favorite pastime and my parents had grown up with a lot of the people still living there. They were trying to make our transition as easy as possible without having neighbors or kids making fun of our situation. We arrived shortly before the bell rang, early enough to see all my new classmates playing in the yard dressed in perfectly pressed uniforms and coordinating accessories. Little girls with long beautiful hair being chased by boys who were laughing and calling out to each other in Spanish–a language that now sounded foreign to me. My parents spoke Spanish to us in our home, but most of the time the words were more commands and yelling. Now, here I was, away from everything I knew as home, away from my friends, and unable to communicate with this culture. My new classmates spoke a Spanish that sounded so beautiful, but they spoke it so fast that I had a difficult time understanding them. Even though my parents Spanish was the same dialect, it still had a different speed and accent that made it hard to understand. A wave of panic came over me as my parents walked away.

I stood in the schoolyard alone, watching the other children. They were as curious about the "new kid" as I was about them. One girl ventured up to me and asked–in English–where I was from.

"The United States," I told her.

She turned to the other kids and yelled, *"Gringa!"*

The other children laughed and high-fived one another. I wasn't sure if I was the butt of a joke or if being a "gringa" was something worthy of celebrating. When the final morning bell rang, the girl that had dubbed me *"Gringa"* grabbed my arm and pulled me to where our other classmates were lining up to begin the day. We stood in perfect order looking up at the beautiful yellow, blue, and red Colombian flag as it waved over the schoolgrounds. The Colombian National Anthem began to play. My classmates sang in unison as I looked around and tried to force myself to feel like I was part of this display of patriotism and national pride. Instead, I felt lost and disconnected. I wanted to go home.

My parents when they were dating

My parents and me

Around age one

At my Abuelita Rosa's front yard in Colombia

My family with my Abuelita Rosa

One of our first trips to the beach in NJ

With the neighborhood pony photographer

Around the time we were deported back to
Colombia

# | 6 |

## MY PURPLE SHOES

*"Dare to reach out your hand into the darkness, to pull another hand into the light"*

– NORMAN B. RICE

———— ❦ ————

My parents tried to acclimate themselves to life in Colombia. My dad drove a taxicab for a while, then became a driver for a "busetta" (which is a smaller version of a regular bus) owned by another of my uncles. But these jobs would be temporary help until he could find a stable job. There were other things he tried, but nothing stuck. We had little money and even less opportunity. The average pay for a professional was less than $200 a month! That was someone with higher education and multiple degrees. My dad's competition for a decent job was impossible to beat. To add to the weight on his shoulders, the whole country was in an uproar. Crime in Medellin was at its highest peak with the most notorious drug lords originating from that city. The cartel was an extremely powerful and dangerous organization that affected the entire country's wellbeing and making it one of the most dangerous countries in the world. Kidnappings were a way for criminals to make fast and big money. Thousands of adults and children were kidnapped to extort their families for money. When families could not afford to pay the ransom, the hostages would be sold into prostitution or illegal markets to different parts of the world.

Had it not been for my grandparents taking us in, we would have been homeless. With all the pressure of my dad not finding work and our welcome slowly expiring, my parents reevaluated our options. We had been in Colombia for a year when my parents decided to risk everything again to try and return to the U.S. I wasn't privy to the planning of our return, but I can imagine the anguish my parents must have felt. It could not have been an easy decision to take their two young daughters to Altar, Mexico, to meet with a "Coyote"–a man who made his living smuggling illegal immigrants across the border. For them to put all our lives at risk, I can only assume that they had exhausted every other possible alternative.

As a parent now, I cannot begin to imagine making a painstaking decision of that magnitude–to accept the risk of death for yourself and your children for a chance at a better life. When you grow up in a place where your needs are met, where there is opportunity to provide for your family, where you are not threatened by violence on a regular basis, it's hard to understand how a parent could accept such a risk. I believe most immigrants would gladly return to their home countries if the same opportunities existed as in the U.S. In a blink of an eye, they would be back with their families, their people, and their culture. When my parents, like so many other immigrants, made the decision to leave their country once again to cross the border into the United States, they did so to give us the chance at a better future.

When the day came to leave Colombia, we rode to the airport with several members of our family. One of my dad's sisters had decided to come with us, leaving her two young boys behind. At the airport, the adults cried and hugged each other tightly, knowing this might be the final goodbye. They knew that nothing would be certain after that moment. All they had was faith. My sister and I didn't know our parent's plan to go to the United States. We thought we were going on a "vacation." As a child, I wasn't allowed to question my parents. I was expected to go where I was told when I was told. But even at such a young age, I sometimes suspected that things were not as they appeared, and as we said goodbye at the airport that day I secretly hoped that we were finally going home. I fantasized that the previous year had been nothing more than a huge misunderstanding and I imagined that my teachers needed me back in class and that my friends missed me. I was ready to go back to where I left off and pretend this experience had never happened.

Those hopes were crumbled when the plane landed and I realized we were in another Spanish-speaking country, a place I did not recognize, where the accent was different, and where most men wore cowboy hats and boots. I remember the way the heat consumed us as we exited the airport. I remember the layer of sweat between my hand and my dad's as he led me into the unknown. I remember feeling confused and anguished. I hoped it was some sort of joke, a mistake. That my dad would fix it, and we would be back on the plane headed to an English-speaking country where the leaves turned orange in the fall. But it wasn't a joke or a mistake. What happened in the weeks that followed would define me in permanent ways.

Don Chui was a burly man in his fifties, a local Coyote who had helped hundreds of immigrants navigate their way through the Mexican desert and across the border into the United States through Phoenix, Arizona. As we exited the airport, we spotted him right away leaning against a white van. He wore a light-blue plaid dress shirt, a cowboy hat, and boots that peeked out from beneath freshly pressed jeans. With a quick wave of two fingers, he motioned for us to come to him. Don Chui's border crossing "travel package" was not cheap. The cost per person in 1985 was $500 per adult and $300 per child. My parents were investing our entire savings, a total of $1,600, on this last-ditch attempt to return to the United States. After a quick debriefing in Spanish about what to expect on this harrowing journey, we were ushered into the van with five others who were also trying to cross the border. One of our traveling companions was a tall, light-skinned man with midnight-black hair and thick mustache. He huddled his teenage son on one side of his body and consoled his two-year-old daughter on the other. From the look on his face, I could tell he was just as nervous as we were.

The smallest of details of that four-day trip are engraved into my memory as if the events had unfolded only yesterday. The hours of walking across dry, scorched earth with the sun beating down on us, the holes in the sand which Don Chui later confirmed were snake holes, the rush to hide when Don Chui thought a patrol was coming, and nights so cold that I can still feel the frigid air biting at my skin. That is how the desert is-brutally hot during the day and bitterly cold as soon as the sun sets. On the coldest night, the adults huddled in what I can only describe as a "human igloo" around the four children in the group to try to keep us warm. Another night, we sat close together under a tree listening to howling wolves that seemed extremely near–an audible reminder of the dangers all around us and how quickly and easily our lives could end.

On yet another night, we took cover in an old brick shed on the property of a local home. The floors of the shed were sand and dirt. Two beat-up, twin-sized iron bed frames formed an "L" shape along two walls. There were no lights, no door, and it was pitch black inside but at least we were sheltered from the weather and dangers. The women and children slept on the bed frames while the men, including Don Chui, sat against the walls huddled shoulder-to-shoulder to keep warm. The room was eerily silent and the only sound was that of nature's sounds. We had barely fallen asleep when Don Chui suddenly jumped to his feet, ran out of the shelter, and screamed for us all to get out. No sooner had we made it outside when Don Chui raised his shotgun and fired into the shed, one shot after another. My tiny body jolted with every squeeze of the trigger. The women were screaming all around me but Don Chui didn't flinch. He lowered his gun and walked back into the shed to retrieve his kill-a rattlesnake. Don Chui ordered everyone back into the shed after he disposed of the rattler's carcass. We did as we were told knowing full well we needed to be well-rested for the long, difficult walk the next morning. The immediate danger was gone thanks to Don Chui's quick reflexes but no one slept that night.

Don Chui knew the desert terrain like the back of his hand. He had made the trip hundreds of times before and he carefully planned each stop along the way. One of those stops was at a stand-alone house in the middle of the desert where we purchased a small sandwich and a soda, rested, and used a real bathroom. As the adults gathered to discuss the remainder of our trip, I wandered off to a window to look outside. Something caught my attention immediately. Under a large tree lay the charred remains of an old car. I was mesmerized. I quietly made my way out of the house and crawled into what was once the driver's seat. As I sat there, I fantasized about all the places I would go if this car were real. *Would I go back to New Jersey to be with my friends? Would I drive to a police station and ask them to tell me why I was in this foreign place? Did they know who Don Chui was? Could someone possibly rescue me from this nightmare?* I would have been content to sit there alone with my thoughts for hours but I was jolted back to reality by a sound in the distance. It was a helicopter. I froze in place and looked over towards the house. My parents were standing at the window frantically waving their hands, motioning at me to get down on the floor. I did not understand their panic but knew better than to ignore them. I had gotten used to the routine of down, tuck, hide, and be silent. I crawled under what was left of the car's flooring, stuffing myself into a tiny crevice under the dashboard. The car began to vibrate as the helicopter drew nearer and a small dust cloud began to rise around the car. Then, as quickly as it appeared, the helicopter lifted higher into the sky and disappeared in the distance. I remained still folded in half like a pretzel with my chapped lips against my knees and my eyes shut tight. When the adults were sure the danger had passed, they rushed to the car screaming at me for putting everyone at risk. My mother slapped me around as if to make emphasis of her parental disapproval and that was the last time I left my parents' side.

On the last day of our journey, Don Chui took us to an area where we met one of his subcontracted men. This man was who would drive us the rest of the way in his pale blue Ford Gran Torino. He was the one who would literally take us across the border. The ingredients of that day included sixteen nervous people, one Ford, one Don Chui, one driver and a heap of prayer. One by one we were jammed into the interior of the vehicle like sausages. Night had fallen and we would be on the other side of life's greatest opportunity within an hour or so. The ride was bumpy and relatively quiet. I was sitting on my mother's lap by the window behind the driver watching the dust swirl and dance along the car side in whimsical artistry. They would create beautiful images of abstract art that represented musical pitches both high and low. I imagined the swirls collaborating with every note of a melody I could dance to. Letting my mind turn into child's play felt so comforting yet so delusional. But the hum of the car with the music video playing outside of my window had me in a trance. Amid my playful imagination, I was startled out of my hypnotic dream when the car came to a screeching halt, the car tail swerving from side to side just two miles into Phoenix, Arizona where it was still darkness and desert. The plan was that the driver would take us just a few more miles into the city and drop us off where we could find a hotel to spend the night. We had made it! Or so we thought.

"*Bajensen Ya!*" The driver was yelling for us to "get out now!"

All hell broke loose as everyone scrambled to get out of the car. My mother quickly pushed me from her lap and slid across the seat towards the other door. I scooted towards her on my right and was almost out of the vehicle when I realized I had lost a shoe. This was not just any shoe. This was one of my favorite purple shoes that had been given to me as a birthday gift from a dear uncle. Those shoes were one of very few gifts I had received in my life and I cherished them dearly. I loved everything about those shimmery shoes. They made me feel like a princess despite living a pauper's life. In my young mind, it was worth saving. It only took a few seconds to find my shoe on the floor and slip it back on but by the time I turned around to continue getting out the car, I had a rifle in my face with a screaming officer on the other end of it. The others had scattered and were hiding in nearby bushes except my mother and two of the other children from the group. My mother was face-down on the ground just feet away from the car. An officer stood over her screaming at her in English. I yelled to him in perfect English that she only spoke Spanish and I offered to translate. The officers were stunned. They asked why I spoke such fluent English,

"I don't belong here. We are just trying to get back home.," I told them.

With my mother, my sister and me in the hands of the authorities, my dad had no choice but to come out of hiding. He raised his hands above his head to indicate his surrender. The others made a run for it. My family and I were arrested along with the young boy that had been traveling with his dad and little sister. In the moments before my dad was to surrender, the boy's dad had given him the address and phone number where he could be reached in the U.S. The man had made an agonizing decision. He felt he could be more helpful to his son by continuing to his destination rather than risk being arrested and sent back. My dad promised to care for his boy until they could be reunited.

We soon learned that the officers who detained us were members of the Native American Indian tribe the Tohono O'odham. Their reservation spans southern Arizona into the northern Mexican town of Sonora. Honestly, I am not sure if they were patrolling the border or we were just unlucky enough to have been trespassing on their land but either way, they detained us and took us to their reservation. When we arrived, we were given sardine sandwiches to eat while we sat around a campfire being questioned by the tribe's chief. After about an hour, the chief instructed his officers to hand us over to U.S. Immigration in Tucson who had arrived for us. From there, we were sent to San Diego and housed at the Travelator Motor Hotel, a makeshift holding facility for immigrants right across the street from the iconic Cortez Hotel.

The facility was not what I expected to see. I thought we would walk into a dimly lit, grungy building and be placed in cells with double bunk beds. I thought everyone would be wearing uniforms surrounded by correctional officers implementing order. Instead, the Travelator looked like a cheap motel with a center courtyard and three floors of wrapping walkways lined by doors. Men were assigned to the top two levels and all women and children were given rooms on the first level. My dad was sent up to join the men on the third floor and my mother and kids were directed towards a room on the first level. The room was clean, had four beds, a couple of nightstands and a shower! It also had a window that had been infilled with brick with a touch of Martha Stewart curtain hanging in front of it. After a long shower and washing away days of dust, dirt and fear, I went over to an empty bed and melted inside the softness of feeling bedsheets again. The young boy traveling with us was a minor so he was told to stay with us. When we walked into the room he bee-lined to the bed closest to the brick window, sat curling his knees up to his chest and tucked his face inside his legs. He sat in this position and rocked himself in muffled sobs for the remainder of the night.

Food was served three times a day. This was an opportunity to reunite with my dad as they allowed families to have meals together. We would meet him in the courtyard and make the line to a cafeteria where they served colorless mush and odorless globs of food. I can still taste the salted water and mystery meat floating in the middle of the bowls they called soup. My dad somehow managed to muster up a smile and cook up a joke or two when we sat to eat. He tried to make light of the situation. I guess in the attempt to disguise our failure, all he had to share was his sense of humor. After dinner, we would be allowed to congregate with others in the courtyard for an hour or so. Then we would be sent back into our rooms.

Even though at the time being detained by immigration was not one of the best experiences in the world, I now feel fortunate to have at least been treated like a human being. Within the confines of our detainment, I recall officers having compassion and extending a hand if any of the detainees needed assistance. I remember the guard at the front door to the cafeteria who would always smile at us kids and wave hello with his fingers. His kindness made those days there, just a little easier to endure. It is gut wrenching to see the deplorable and inhumane conditions with which detained immigrants are treated today. No access to maintain their hygiene, children sleeping on concrete floors being ripped away from their parents—most of whom will tragically be lost in the system and probably never see their parents again. Adults forced to stand for days on end because they are crammed 900 to a cage like animals instead of human lives. Literally watching humans die while under the care of the richest country in the world is despicable and embarrassing. In the U.S., there are laws prohibiting violence or cruelty against animals and we seem to enforce those laws more than we do respecting our foreign neighbors. It truly tears me in half to witness this act of savagery! Especially as I resonate with my fellow immigrants whose mere crime is to dare to dream of a better life.

Although it seemed like an eternity, after four days of being detained we were given two options: go back to Colombia or pay a five-figure fine and be placed with a host family in New Jersey. Knowing we had nothing to return to in Colombia and given the opportunity to finally achieve the American Dream, we went with option two. Our family back in Colombia scrambled together their savings to help us stay in America. Once the fine was paid, the doors to our freedom opened before us and we were released.

I was finally back "home" in New Jersey. A wonderful host family welcomed us with open arms. They sponsored our stay, helped secure employment for my dad and they also arranged to have us reunite with my little brothers who had been staying in the U.S. with friends. The family gave me a shiny metallic pink bomber jacket to welcome me back to America. Things should have been good but the trauma of what had transpired during our trip through the desert and our capture in Arizona continued to haunt me. One day I overheard my parents emotionally recounting the details of how we'd been caught to the host family. My mother saw me eavesdropping and pointed at me while she cried,

*"Por culpa de esta culicagada!" It's this little shitter's fault!* she yelled.

My mother blamed the entire failed border crossing and our subsequent imprisonment experience on me because I went back to retrieve my purple shoe. I am still unsure of her thought process or lack thereof to put such a horrendous burden on the shoulders of her little girl. I carried the weight of this accusation well into my adulthood. That blame framed me as the bad guy in our family's story and I paid the price for it with my extended family in Colombia as well. Worst off, I accepted the blame and I too believed I was the bad guy and that it had been my fault. Because of it, I associated purple with my guilt and shame and swore never to use it again. I was repulsed by the color and I was repulsed with myself.

In February 2017, I was invited to fulfill a dream of sharing my story on the infamous TEDx Talk platform at JWU Miami. A few months before I delivered my talk, "When Breaking Points Lead to

Empowerment" and as I wrote my speech, I knew the time had come to make peace with myself, to forgive the little girl that dragged around a life-long anchor that did not belong to her, to tell her that she was not the bad guy and that any guilt associated with it would be absolved. I understood that in an act of desperation and pain, I became my mother's scapegoat, but the time had come to exonerate that little girl and to allow her to walk proudly. Just as my mother did, I also used a scapegoat. I blamed myself and I used the color purple to associate with that culpability. But my story was to be told from the position of healing, of forgiveness and of strength and that also included finally releasing that little girl from her penalty. I was ready to clean my slate and liberate my guilt.

The morning of my Tedx Talk, as I rehearsed one last time before walking out the door, I slipped into my off-white blazer, tucked one side of my hair behind my ear, proudly slipped into my purple stiletto heels and slowly walked in front of the mirror. As I took one deep breath in, I looked up at my reflection and started my speech... "I was fourteen years old when I received my last beating..."

My first professional photo in the U.S.

# | 7 |

# WRONG PLACE - WRONG TIME

*"The world breaks everyone and afterward many are strong at the broken places"*

– ERNEST HEMINGWAY

———— ❦ ————

Have you ever made a decision that seemed great at the time, but you later come to regret it? This was the case for my parents when they listened to the advice of family who suggested we get a fresh start in Florida. One of my uncles had relocated there from Colombia a few years prior and raved about living in paradise, and more importantly, about the opportunities for work and building a stable life. We moved to Kendall, Florida, into my uncle's spacious four-bedroom rental home. At first, it really did seem like paradise. The home was a palace to me. Glass doors in the living spaces and a kitchen facing the underground pool. Endless palm trees in the backyard and a lake behind the property. My siblings and I spent countless hours watching cartoons each morning and I even liked my new school.

Unlike the old-fashioned feel of the school back in New Jersey, Florida offered a fun outdoor education that was fascinating. We would walk from trailer to trailer to go to class, and each time I stepped outside I would turn my face to the sun and breathe in the scent of the fragrant flowers blooming throughout the property. We would eat lunch under a tree with my entire class sitting Indian style as we laughed and ran our fingers through the grass. I felt like I had finally found a sense of normalcy. My parents were even arguing less. In the afternoons, we would often go to Mark Twain's Riverboat Playhouse, an indoor amusement center in Kendall Lakes, with my uncle's girlfriend and her daughter who is also named Erika, herein referenced as her nickname "Ellie". She was a bright little girl with an untainted and lighthearted spirit. Life was finally looking up. I felt certain that all the pain and sadness was over, and the memories of the past would slowly be replaced with happy ones.

One day, our whole family was home. My mother was in the kitchen washing dishes. My dad and all the kids were consumed with a very intense game of hide and go seek. Absconded in a perfect hiding spot behind the living room curtains, I waited, giggling softly as my sister, who was "it" began her seeking. There was a knock at the front door. My uncle and his girlfriend had gone out to watch a sports game and wouldn't be back for hours, so I knew it wasn't them. The knock got sharper and sounded urgent, so I came out of my hiding place and ran towards the door. As I slowly opened the door, confronting me was a sea of uniforms framed by flashing lights from several police cars parked in front of my uncle's house. The officer in charge positioned one hand on his handgun holster, waived a piece of paper in my face with the other and ordered me to answer, "Where are you parents?"

My uncle and his girlfriend were escorted into the house in handcuffs as countless police officers poured in, screaming at my mother to get on the ground and put her hands behind her head. A female officer corralled the kids and told us to stay still near the tv area. I watched as my dad was dragged out of the back bedroom by two officers. He was handcuffed and thrown face down on the living room floor next to my mother who was sobbing in prayer. For hours, the officers ransacked the entire house, flipping furniture upside down, tearing open cushions and framed artwork, emptying cabinets, and letting the contents fall to the ground and break. Finally, the confused and crying children were escorted out of the house into one police car and the adults in handcuffs into others. A caravan of sirens drowned out the screams of my siblings, the rattling walkie-talkies, and the panicked cries of adults being pushed into cars as shocked neighbors looked on and the strobe of police lights departed our cul-de-sac.

My uncle had gotten caught up in some bad decisions with some pretty bad people, and as a result, everyone within his circle was caught up in the mix. That night four adults were arrested and sent to jail and five children were detained by child services. Another broken home. Within hours, we were all in different facilities. Ellie was signed over to her mother's family, but they only had room to take in two more kids, so they took in my two younger brothers. My sister and I were sent to a temporary orphanage in the pits of Hialeah that housed children of incarcerated parents. Once again, my life was another shattered dream.

The house we were taken to was musky and dark. We were given our own room with two twin-sized beds which also had the infamous brick-filled window. We were allowed in the living room only when told and with supervision. We would be woken up before the sun at 4:30 a.m. to take a shower and clean up. By 5:30 a.m. we had to be at the dining table eating breakfast quietly while the lady in charge served all the children. There were three other kids in the house with us who seemed more accustomed to this ritual than the scared, wide-eyed little girls we were. At breakfast I choked down my lukewarm pancakes seasoned by the salty tears that rolled down my face.

We had a scheduled playtime during the day when we could go outside and play with generations-old, rusty toys in the front yard of the house. I hardly ever played with anything but often pressed myself up against the fence that faced the main street to stare at the McDonald's a few blocks away. I would fantasize my escape to coincide with the sitting attendant's afternoon nap. I could always tell when she was about to doze off. She would cross her arms over her big bosom and nestle her chin into them. At that moment, I dreamed I would jump over the fence and run as fast as I could to that McDonald's. I would burst through the door and explain to anyone who would listen that I had been taken away from my parents–that I had no idea where they were and I would beg for help to find them. Of course, I never escaped. Fear paralyzed my twiggy little legs and the attendant would usher us back into the house after her snoring startled her awake.

While at that house, I spent most of my time in the bedroom staring endlessly at a dimly lit light bulb hung from the ceiling. There was nothing exciting to do in the room, but it beat sitting in the common area with the boring caretakers. One day as I lay on my bed, I was startled by muffled voices I heard coming from the small closet in the bedroom. I shot up out of bed and stood in front of the closet leaning my ear against the door. Then I heard a lady's laugh clearly coming from inside the closet! I thought I was losing my mind, but I decided to investigate further. I opened the closet door and sat on the floor. Sure enough, the voices of two women came through the wall. Instinctively, I investigated and began tracing the wall with my hands. I could feel unfinished drywall slightly tugging at my fingertips and then I stopped at what felt like a trace of an opening. As I allowed my fingers to follow the outline, my heart started to race faster. As I continued to investigate, I came across a door clip. I stopped, looked back into the room to make sure no one else was watching me and when I lightly pulled at the clip, the wall slowly pushed in.

At first, I thought I was imagining this but as I continued to push the wall, I was able to crawl into a room. As I slowly rose to my feet, I began to take in the space. There were desks and computers and printers pushing out papers. The distant melody of an awesome 80's song played on the radio as the aroma of freshly brewed coffee wafted through the air. With short steps, I moved cautiously beyond the doorway and into another room. As I entered the next room, I saw two women talking as they pointed at one of the monitors on their desk. As they were deeply engrossed in discussion, I stood there motionless trying to decide whether I wanted them to see me or not. I straightened my spine and laced my fingers and properly folded them in front of me. I could hear myself breathing but I tried not to make a noise. To my horror my stomach emitted a muffled rumble that vibrated around the room. Instantly both ladies turned around. I am not sure who was the most startled–the ladies when they saw me standing there or me trying to make sense of this world on the other side of the closet!

Both women were in their thirties' and possibly Hispanic. They wore professional suits and impressive heels. One had beautiful black hair that was long and shiny. She was dressed in a grey business skirt, a white tucked in blouse and shiny black high heels. She walked quickly over to me and held me by my shoulders. She glanced over my head to try and make sense of where I had come from. Quickly she realized I had found the hidden closet door that led into the administrative offices of the orphanage. Not intended for daily use, the hidden door was to be used in case of emergencies. Now that I had found it, the ladies had to make sure that I wouldn't use it again. They quickly ushered me to one of the chairs. One bombarded me with questions as the other picked up the phone to frantically dial the caretakers next door. She asked me if I knew where I was, who they were, what my name was. I replied that I didn't know where my parents were and that I had been taken away from them against my will by police officers.

I remember thinking this was as good a chance as any to plead for my freedom! I started begging and pleading to her to adopt me. I knew that if my parents had been taken away in handcuffs by police officers, they had been taken to jail. And I knew that jail was not some place you went in and came out of easily. For all I knew, my parents would be gone forever and someone would eventually adopt me so why not her. I remember grabbing her hands and imploring; "I promise I will behave. I'll help around the house. I'll clean whatever needs to be cleaned. I'll do good in school. Just please take me with you." I told her I didn't want to be there anymore. I just wanted to be in a normal home and have a normal life. I swore I would never be a nuisance and she'd like me. I begged. I supplicated. I cried. I felt her hands slowly slide out from mine as she brought one of them up to her face to wipe the tears welling up in her eyes. The other lady hung up the phone and rapidly walked towards us. They each dragged a chair to each side of me and sat down. After taking a few breaths and looking at each other, they turned to me and explained that they also didn't know where my parents were but promised that I would see them again soon. They explained that I couldn't be adopted because I still belonged to my parents. They assured me that my parents were probably as sick with worry about me as I was about them. I remember thinking, *You don't know my parents.* I just wanted a normal kid's life. I was tired of the ups and downs of the roller coaster life I had been living. I just wanted to be back in Christopher Columbus School #15 in Ms. Coakley's class learning about pronouns and adverbs. I would have given anything to close my eyes and go back to the days of sitting in the cafeteria peeling back the aluminum foil of free lunches filled with steaming hot spaghetti and meatballs. Instead here I sat in front of two women staring at me with sadness and telling me there was nothing they can do, that I had to go back next door and behave until my parents came to get me. I crumbled in my chair and my soul hit the floor. Their voices faded into mumbles as my mind raced ahead. I knew they would take me back to the secret closet door and I'd be back staring at the bare light bulb in the ceiling in my room wondering what would happen next.

After a while, they both stood up and helped me to my feet. I, feeling defeated and unwanted, heard one of them say as they slowly walked me towards the closet door, "Erika, I am so sorry you are in this situation but you cannot open that door again. Remember that everything is going to be okay. You will see your parents soon and your life will be normal again." As we approached the door, the lady holding my hand turned me to face her. She stooped to bring her face down to my level and with a soft voice said, "Erika... I promise everything is going to be okay. Do you believe me?" She stared into my eyes looking for a sign that I believed her. Instead she found tears welling up on my lids and then plunging down my little face. With one stroke of her right hand she gently wiped the stream of tears off my cheeks. Then she handed me a white box and smiled. As I slowly received the box, my tears falling hard against the top of it, she asked me to open it. Confused I examined the contents which were remnants of sewing material, a tanned stocking, a ball of cotton, and a pretty pink doll dress that had white lacing stitched to the collar. There was a thick needle and sewing thread and a booklet with instructions for what appeared to be a sew-it-yourself rag doll kit.

She told me that she was giving me this as a gift to keep me busy while I was staying at the orphanage. "By the time you finish making this doll, I promise you'll be back home with your parents." She then softly replaced the lid and handed the box back to me. Both of them bent down to give me a tight hug and then one of them opened the closet door. She said, "It was very nice to meet you Erika. Remember that everything is going to work out just fine. Build your doll and you'll soon be home." I looked back into the closet and noticed one of the caretakers was waiting for me on the other side looking displeased with my behavior. I took a few tentative steps into the closet and then inside the bedroom. As the caretaker held my shoulders in place, I turned around to see the ladies peeking through the door. Once I was on the other side, they sadly smiled and waved goodbye. The last thing I saw was the lady with the pretty black hair giving me a thumbs up as she closed the door.

**My siblings and me when we lived in Florida**

# | 8 |

# INNOCENCE LOST

*"There are wounds that never show on the body that are deeper and more hurtful than anything that bleeds."*

– LAURELL K. HAMILTON

———— ❧ ————

When Ellie's family realized my parents were going to be in jail longer than expected, they decided to make room to take my sister and I into their home. I was glad to be reunited with my siblings and with Ellie, but one of the things that made me happiest while I was living there was hanging out with Ellie's "Auntie C". She was young and fun and full of energy. Auntie C did not live in the home but would occasionally stop by and take Ellie, my sister and me for a ride in her sports car. She'd play any music we asked for, and the four of us would sing and laugh as we zoomed around town. I was twelve at the time, the oldest of the three girls, and I loved spending time with her.

One evening, Auntie C stopped by as she had done many times before, but this night would not be like any other night of my life. The plan was to go to the mall and get ice cream, but first we had to pick up one of Auntie C's friends. We turned into a community of tidy-looking homes and pulled into an empty parking space. Auntie C's friend was standing outside of her front door eagerly waving hello. When we got out of the car, she gave Auntie C a big hug and patted each of our heads softly then escorted us into her home. It was spacious and immaculate and smelled of potpourri. She led us down a corridor into a living area where her husband was sitting on a plush sofa, cradling a tiny baby who swaddled in a white blanket. The baby's tiny head was the only thing visible. The dad lovingly rocked the baby from side to side and flashed us with a dazzling smile. He was a tall, tanned Latino man with gel-slicked hair and dark, prominent eyebrows.

The adults gathered in the living room, sharing small talk while we patiently waited by Auntie C's side. I was already thinking ahead to the ice cream. I was going to ask for my favorite rocky road with melted marshmallow syrup in a waffle cone. This delicious treat was going to make my night. The husband walked away briefly into one of the interior rooms and came back without the baby. He talked with his wife and Auntie C convincing them they would get a lot more done if they left the kids behind. After debating it for a few minutes, the ladies agreed with the man and Auntie C turned to us to promise ice cream on another day and said she would bring us back some goodies from the mall. With no more than a tap on our heads, a warning to behave, and a quick smile, Auntie C and her friend waved goodbye and left.

After walking the ladies to the front door, the husband returned to the living room, rubbing his hands as he bent down to our height. "How about a game of hide and seek," he suggested with a smile. "We are going to have so much fun!" He pointed at my sister and said, "You're it," guiding her to a corner to count to twenty. As she started her countdown, Ellie looked around for the perfect hiding spot and headed towards the front of the house. The husband, who was now standing next to me, grabbed my hand and said, "Come, you'll hide with me." He led me to a bedroom at the end of the hallway and closed the door behind us. The baby was sleeping peacefully in the middle of a king-size bed. The room was small and cramped with bulky, over-sized furniture making it feel claustrophobic. There was a TV in front of the bed which he flipped on as he sat down on the edge of the bed. "Don't be scared. Come, sit here," he said, motioning for me to join him. I was uncomfortable, but my twelve-year-old brain tried to make sense of the situation. Maybe he wanted to play this game and watch his baby at the same time, I reasoned. Maybe because I was the oldest, he needed my help. He patted the bed again and called me over to him a second time. At that point, my stomach turned upside down. I felt a chill on my skin and although the moment felt extremely uncomfortable and wrong, I was praying that I was reading more into it than what it was. As he patted the bed, I obeyed him and slowly walked to the other corner at end of the bed and sat down leaving ample space between us.

"We can watch TV while your sister looks for us," he said casually, turning to face the television.

I really was not comfortable with watching TV in that setting but it didn't seem there was much else to do than to sit and watch TV. I can't tell you what was on the screen though because all I was focusing on was trying to quiet the screaming in my head and the thumping of my heart pounding against my chest. My hands were clammy with sweat but my body had a chill that caused me to slightly shiver. My throat felt like it was closing up and dry and I began to feel lightheaded. With fear pounding in my chest, all I can remember thinking was how long would it take my sister to find us. The minutes seemed to feel like hours. I refused to look in his direction hoping that would discourage him from wanting to engage in conversation but instead he inched his way closer to me. A jolt of fear raced down my spine which startled my body upright. He laughed.

"Don't be so scared," he said. "We're just watching TV."

I began to feel nauseated, the same feeling you get in the pit of your stomach when you're at the top of a roller coaster waiting for it to drop and you know what's coming but you're strapped in and can't get out. Not a moment later he put his hand on my shoulder and quickly laid me on my back. The baby's feet innocently brushed against the top of my head. My legs dangled off the edge of the bed. I focused my eyes on the ceiling fan above that was spinning furiously like the thoughts rushing through my brain. He climbed on top of me, crushing me under his weight. He ran his hands up and down the sides of my body and breathed heavily against my neck, sniffing me like a dog. I jerked my face away from him, too terrified to move, too terrified to call for help. I could barely breathe. Surely it was just a bad dream and any minute I would wake up. I froze as he ran his hands over places that no twelve-year-old's body should be touched–at first over my clothes and then inside them. Then, I heard myself scream.

He pinned his hardened body furiously against mine and muffled my mouth with one hand. He then jerked one hand over my breasts, and as he threatened me to shut up, he used his other hand to pry my thighs open. I whimpered helplessly. As he continued to wrestle me into position, I started to fight back his every move with all the strength I had. We physically struggled for what seemed an eternity then somehow I felt a burst of courage and strength surged through my body. From deep within, the potency of my voice roiled its way up to my throat and I wailed louder than ever as I flailed my arms and legs kicking and screaming underneath him! As he tried to control my wildness, I scratched him deeply wherever my nails could find skin. In the struggle however, one of my legs freed up from underneath his leg and I thrusted my knee against his scrotum with all the force I could muster leaving him coiled and gasping for air. I was not going to let this happen to me! Not without a fight for my life. As he slid sideways on the bed still cradling his scrotum, I frantically jumped up and ran toward the door only to find it locked.

He laughed and threatened, "You better not tell anybody," as I struggled to unlock the door. He slowly sat up and mockingly rubbed his penis into place and said, "No one will believe you anyway." I unlocked the door and threw it open just as my sister was coming out of the bathroom across the hall from the bedroom. I grabbed her by the arm and nervously dragged her to the living room. I sat her and I on the sofa and warned her she was not to leave my side from that point forward. Confused, she looked at me and said she did not understand what I was doing. "Just stay still and sit with me," I ordered. That man remained in the bedroom only occasionally coming out to check and see what we were doing. He'd look at us on the sofa, smirk, walk back into his bedroom and shut the door. Ellie, who had already found something else to play with in the living room, came by us and sat on the floor. We all sat in the living room as I tried to swallow the knot in my throat and hold my shaking body in place until the women returned a few hours later.

The ride back to the house was long, painful, and lonely. I sat quietly in the back seat staring at the menacing palm trees and flickering streetlights as the rest of the girls sang and laughed with Auntie C. My head was numb. I felt filthy and the knot in my throat prevented me from breathing normally. I wanted to take a shower as soon as I got back to the house but wasn't sure that would wash away the filthy feeling on my body. Noting my silence, and the lack of my engagement with the car concert, my sister poked me on the shoulder and asked, "What's wrong?" I glared at her at first but figured I should at least tell her so I began telling her everything quietly so Auntie C or Ellie wouldn't hear. I needed to get it out. I needed someone to help me figure out what to do because I felt completely lost. But telling my sister turned out to be a mistake as I was crushed by her response. "You better not tell anyone," she warned me. She shrugged and added: "You're probably making it up anyway. You just want attention." And just like that, she turned away from me and picked up where she left off singing with the girls. I felt as if I had been violated again remembering his threat, "No one will believe you anyway."

I never told anyone else what happened that night. I believed what I had been told, first by the monster who violated me and then by my own sister. *No one will believe you!* He was right. As I did with all the other painful memories I carried, I decided to bury this deep inside and never think of it again. I would force myself to forget that night, the stupid game of hide-and-seek, the molestation, and the pain.

A few weeks later, Ellie's mom took us to visit my mother in jail. The coldness of the institution was beyond scary. The walls were as grey and cold as the ugliest winter sky in New Jersey. The walls seemed to purposely cave into you as you waited in the lobby amongst hundreds of locals standing around to visit women inmates. Every few minutes, a correction officer would come out of a big metal door and start screaming out names at which point people would stand up and quickly walk towards her as she guided them into the visiting rooms. Some of these people looked like they belonged inside the cells rather than in the waiting room with us. When they finally called our names, we walked towards the big burly officer as she greeted us with a unibrow frown on her face showing us she was not about playing games. We quietly followed her as she led us to the partitioned enclosures where we can see my mother. Her hair in a lopsided afro and the wrinkles around her eyes significantly more pronounced than I had remembered. She looked like she had been crying for weeks. Her outfit matching the same grey as the walls. As we crammed into the partition, she sat opposite us behind a clear wall and lifted a handset off the side of her partition. Ellie's mom repeated the same behavior on our side. We didn't get to speak with my mother as you could only hear her through the phone headset that Ellie's mom used. At times, they both cried and at times my mother seemed to beg her to help. I just stared at my mother in shock seeing her so helpless and vulnerable. And just as quickly as we had sat down, an officer came up behind her, tapped her on the shoulder, and motioned her to follow her. The visit had ended and we were escorted to leave. That was the only time I visited my mother in jail.

Months later, my parents were cleared of any involvement with my uncle's business and the authorities confirmed we were a casualty of being at the wrong place at the wrong time. They were released, and we were all reunited. We rented an apartment in Hialeah while my parents tried to figure out their next steps. Our apartment was on the first floor and had a direct view of the community tennis courts. We only had a few furnishings but enough to get us by, and I made a few friends in the complex while we were there. Overall, things were okay. But of course, that wouldn't last.

One afternoon, I was in my room, lying on my bed with my eyes closed, listening to my Walkman. Music had become a great escape for me and I spent hours on end unplugged from everything but 80's music. I had the volume turned up as loud as I my headphones could handle and was enjoying the rhythm of the base thumping in my ears when my sister barged in and slapped me on the leg. "What do you want?" I barked after taking off my headset.

"Oh... you're in trouble! My mom and dad are calling you!"

In the living room, my mother was crying hysterically at the dining table. My dad was silent, fists balled up at his sides, trying hard to stifle his rage as he paced throughout the living space. I turned down the music on my Walkman and looked at my parents then at my sister.

"I told them." my sister said to me matter-of-factly.

At first, I didn't understand what she meant. *Did she tell them I was blasting my Walkman? Did she tell them I was in a bad mood again? What had she told them? And why was everyone freaking out?* My dad grabbed my arm and began shaking me violently, demanding that I tell him what happened with *the man at the house.* My Walkman fell off my belt clip and hit the floor, and my unplugged headphones were dangling around my neck. My mother kept screaming for me to answer *"YA!"- NOW!*

My sister watched with a smirk on her face as my parents yanked and slapped me around, demanding answers. I was terrified and embarrassed. *What could I say? What did they want to hear? That the monsters' hands had violated my body? That it had not been my fault? That I had escaped what could have been a traumatic rape because I was brave enough to use my voice to scream and my knee to kick? Why weren't they proud of my survival efforts instead of being angry?* But all these questions went unanswered. I said nothing because there were no good answers, and nothing I said could have prevented the beating I received that night. I was beaten "because I had lied." I was beaten "because I hadn't told them what happened with that man." And I was beaten "because the only reason I would keep a secret like that was because I probably looked for it and I liked it."

My parents were incapable of offering me compassion at a moment when they themselves felt out of control and violated. Possibly by me. Possibly by that man. Possibly by the sequence of events brought on by relocating to Florida and then incarceration. Regardless of the why, they chose to unleash their fury and indignation on the only thing they felt they could control... me.

My parents insisted on taking me to a medical facility to be examined as a rape victim. I was petrified and protested that I had not been raped. I told the doctor that the man had touched my breasts and my vagina with his hands, but I had freed myself before he could do any more harm. I begged them to believe me, but it was no use. I was interrogated and pressed to retell my story in excruciating detail to strangers and forced to undergo an examination in which every orifice of my young body was poked and prodded to search for signs of sexual assault. Only then did I truly feel I had been raped. Raped of value. Raped of the truth. And raped of my voice.

My parents had made the journey to Florida in hopes of a better life, a new start and the possibility of progressing as a family. Instead, they now had criminal records attached to their names, more painful memories to bury and a responsibility to reestablish a broken family yet again. The move to Florida had brought worse struggles than any we had in New Jersey. It was inevitable that they would decide to move back. My parents packed up the few belongings we had and within days, we hit the road northbound. Elizabeth, New Jersey would become our home again.

# | 9 |

# THE DAY GOD ANSWERED

*"You can either be a host to God, or a hostage to your ego."*

– DR. WAYNE DYER

———— ⌘ ————

We had not been back in New Jersey long. It was an ordinary night, if you dare call my life ordinary, still around age twelve. I had spent the better part of my night watching MTV music videos trying to cheer up. Billy Idol had just romanced my screen with "Eyes Without a Face" and Madonna was about to serenade me with an iconic rendition of "Live to Tell".

Before we left Florida, my parents were able to salvage some of the furniture that had been confiscated in the house raid and packed a moving truck with the belongings to head back north. Fitting a bunch of odds and ends furniture pieces into a small studio apartment with four children and two adults became quite the undertaking. The living room opened to the bedroom area and an enclosed porch at the front of the house. The porch was just big enough to squeeze a twin-size mattress into it, so it was used as a second bedroom. The living area became a Lego-like storage unit stacked with furniture that did not fit anywhere–a dresser, topped with a sofa, topped with another sofa on one wall. Pressed up against the opposite wall was another twin-size bed. The only other thing that fit in the room was a small TV on a small stand perched awkwardly in front of the windows and surrounded by piles of garbage everywhere. There was a one-foot strip of walking space that led from one area to the other.

I felt overwhelmed and sad that night. My parents had fought all day and my siblings had followed suit bickering with each other. My only pet, a black cat called PJ that I received as a gift from a school friend, Miriam, had now been missing for weeks and everything about the apartment evoked gloom. The room was dark as I now lay there staring at the ceiling and searching for the answers to all of life's questions. But in the stillness of that night and lost in thought, I started to think about something I had never really put thought to before. God.

Our religious upbringing had been hypocritical at best. We were never really taught our beliefs or what being "Catholic" meant but we were very much Catholic when we were asked. We would rush into church late on any random Sunday, but especially on Easter, where we sat there motionless to listen to the priest talk for an hour and a half. We duplicated the same robotic motions as the entire congregation during the service and then went home. Every now and then, we would be sent to catechism class and were expected to somehow pick up some spirituality or fear of God, whichever came first. We would quietly sit and listen while they read from the bible and then we would rejoin my parents in church. So naturally the thought of God, to me, was always a God that I was to be afraid of. Throughout my childhood, I felt His wrath and I was no one to question who He was or why He would allow all the misery and unhappiness we experienced. I would sometimes see my mother crying with clasped hands held up to her forehead in pleading agony as she whispered her conversations to Him. But it was obvious He hadn't been listening. And so, I never really understood the power or significance of God other than the fear He invoked in me.

That night, however, I felt curious enough to explore. I sat up and looked around and realized I was by myself. My mother was in the kitchen listening to a talk show on the radio and my siblings were on the kitchen floor at her feet playing. My dad had returned to his Saturday night drinking binges to release the "stress of his work week". In the silence of my moment, I thought, what if I wasn't afraid to talk to God. *What if I tried to talk to Him and He answered back! Hey! What if I told Him what was going on with us and He'd be able to help! What would that meeting look like?* Without skipping a beat, I rose out of bed and ran to the bathroom. I took a shower, washed my hair, combed it nicely and then put it in a side braid. I put on body lotion and clipped my finger and toenails. Then I found a pair of clean pajamas in the pile of balled-up laundry on one of the beds and put them on pressing my hands like irons to straighten out the wrinkles. After brushing my teeth, I hopped back into bed. I knelt like the people I had seen at church, but on top of my bed so my knees wouldn't hurt on the floor. I put my hands together in prayer and I closed my eyes tightly. I figured that if this was going to be my first conversation with God, I was to be clean, properly groomed and poised. He would certainly pay more attention to me if He saw that I had put myself together nicely once I called to Him in prayer.

"Umm... Hi God. I am not sure if you're listening but... Can You hear me? I am not sure if I am supposed to be talking to You or not because we are all afraid of You but I want to ask You for a favor. Can You please change my life? Not sure if You can fix this family or send me away to another one. Any other one would be great actually! I just want a happier life. You know? I don't want this one anymore. I don't want to cry or get hit or go to orphanages anymore. I just want to be happy like my friends are. If You do, I promise I will always obey and be clean, do my bed and wash my hair and clip my nails. I will put on lotion and brush my teeth, and do good in school but, can You please just fix my life?"

I motioned the sign of the cross with two fingers. First on my forehead, then on my chest then on my left shoulder and then the right. I kissed my fingers and tucked myself into bed. I smiled and felt so happy that I had put in my prayers and was surely going to receive them. But for now, I would just be patient and wait.

Months went by and my patience wore thin. God did not answer me. He did not answer me that night nor what it seemed like many nights after that. There was a time when I thought, He could not possibly even be real especially when I looked around this world and saw evil people succeeding and good people suffering. Inevitably with time, I took on the position that evil always won and others just paid the consequences of choosing to do right. I associated my continuous struggles with a burden I carried for doing what was right and carried that weight in my heart alongside spiritual resentment for a long time.

The resentment spread deeper and into my adulthood. I grew angrier at God with each hardship and at times demanded answers for all the cruelty I had been through. I often asked, when was He going to show up to my life and save me? When was it going to start getting easier and when would I get a payoff for all the suffering I had endured? There had been plenty of times when I pulled my car off to the side of the road crying hysterical, punching my steering wheel screaming *DUDE!!! WHAT DID I DO TO DESERVE THIS?!? WHY DO YOU KEEP PUNISHING ME?!?* I had focused my life on doing good for others, on letting go of hatred and resentment only to get wronged more and beaten harder. For a while I felt like He had abandoned me when I needed Him the most and my faith took a toll because of it.

Then one year, in my early twenties, I was having another whaling tantrum in the car. A pretty ugly one at that. I was again on the side of the road, physically exhausted from crying, hyperventilating and screaming and as I was about to go into my typical pity party God rant, I had a strange moment of lucidity. Everything went quit except for the sound of my breathing. Heavily at that, but suddenly I became clearly aware of my breathing. I noticed I had breath. I also noticed I was sitting inside a good car with a full tank of gas where I was dry from the pouring rain unlike those sleeping on the sidewalk next to me. I remembered that in the trunk of my car, I had groceries I was able to purchase to make dinner as I watched a woman dig through a trashcan near the bus stop. As the rain continued to crash against the ceiling of my car, I slowly realized that in my egotistical obsession for always wanting what I didn't have, I was missing the preciousness of all I did have. That maybe the whole concept of God was not physical but was about having faith that all was already being done. Of trusting the journey and letting go of my ego in thinking that it was supposed to be different. Of BELIEVING that my experiences were preparing me for a grander purpose and all was just fine if I dared to see it that way. It finally hit me that just maybe, He had been listening to me and traveling by my side all along. That He had been my guiding light and that no matter how close to the edge I got, there was always His energy that pulled me back. And that even when things were really bad, they could have been worst. That in my rebelliousness and affinity of holding on to my past, I was not living in the beautiful moments of my present.

As the rain began to clear, I felt a wave of inner peace come over me and when I closed my eyes to delve in the moment, I felt loved. I felt safe. I felt cherished. I felt God. I had been so busy demanding of Him that I hadn't been able to see that God had been with me every step of the way. In good times and in bad. That my prayers had been answered and that little girl who once believed, needed to remind her grown up self to just look around her to see it. That day, sitting in my car, God spoke to me. I finally felt His presence and felt the spiritual awakening I had yearned for so long. My life and the world around me seemed to look brighter and my heart felt less betrayed. I understood the profoundness of faith and believing even when I couldn't see it. That letting go of controlling the outcome and just believing that all would be done, would take the weight off my soul. And as I sat in a moment of mercy... I softly whispered... All in His time, not mine.

# | 10 |

## ONE MORE TRY

*"A second chance doesn't mean anything if you didn't learn from your first."*

– ANURAG PRAKASH RAY

---

I spent a few wonderful years living at the Nun's house discovering a new life and evolving into a young adult. Throughout those years, I kept in touch with my dad regularly. We would meet for coffee and he'd give me money for things I needed or update me on how my other siblings were doing. After I ran away from home, my mother forbade all my siblings to talk or see me at all. The only glimpse on knowing how they were was through stories my dad would share or the occasional opportunity he would sneak my brothers out so they can see me for a few minutes during our coffee meet ups. Those were very seldom though as my dad was petrified my mother would find out.

About a year into living at the Nun's house, I started working at a local clothing store to help pay for my own expenses while still attending high school with a goal to graduate. At the end of my second year, one of my roommates said she was moving out with her boyfriend and offered the second bedroom of their new place to me. I thought this was perfect! A great opportunity for me to go live the real adult life and I quickly packed my bags, thanked the Nuns and moved out. After I moved out, I told my dad. Even though my dad understood that my life with the Nun's was a good change for me from the situation back at home, when he found out I moved out to another place... he was not happy at all. Deep down inside, I think he yearned for me to come back home and put all that had happened behind us. Every time I would see him, he would bring up my mother and how distraught she was of this situation and how she secretly wanted me back. I never really knew if that was him embellishing or if it was the truth. Either way, I was not interested in going back to my past. I was happy with the new outlook of my life.

But one day, during another coffee meet up, he was particularly insistent that I give my mother another chance. He said we could take it slow but that I should try to rekindle my relationship with her. One of my dad's personality traits is not letting go until he achieves the impossible and so I conceded to speak to my mother again just so he would drop the topic.

As you can imagine, the first meeting was awkward at best. My dad escorted me back into the house as if he were bringing home the long-lost daughter and my mother was sitting in the living room waiting. It had been three years since I had run away from this very home and walking back in made me feel a multitude of emotions. I felt oddly more empowered but also like a stranger in that house. However, the memories were still overwhelmingly fresh, and I felt uneasy. I slowly walked in, shyly waved my hand hello and sat on the sofa nearest the door. My mother corresponded with a short hello as she sat stoic on her side. My dad sat in as the standing referee as he prompted the beginning of our conversation.

We made small talk and we both avoided the elephant in the room. She asked how I was doing, and I was brief with my answers leaving out details. But then my brothers ran in and threw themselves on me for an explosive hug and we giggled in our embrace. My dad then shared stories on how they had been behaving and what they had been up to as my mother would chime in periodically. I could see how happy this reunion made my dad especially as he saw how my brothers would fight over each other for my attention as they would tell me stories of what they did that day. In some odd way, the reunion also made me extremely happy because I missed my brothers terribly.

As the weeks went by, my dad would occasionally invite me to swing by the house to see my siblings and I would bring them gifts whenever I could afford them. The three years I missed out on growing up with them really pained me. My visits became more frequent as I continued to make up for time lost with my little brothers. My mother kept me at a guarded distance whenever I would visit, and I reciprocated with the same sentiment. I ignored what seemed to be a continuously growing problem with my mother's hoarding and the fighting between her and my dad. I made a decision that those weren't my problems anymore since I didn't live there. Besides, I was only making the efforts to go back for my dad and my two little brothers.

One day, though, I went by the house and as soon as I arrived, my mother asked me to take her to the hospital because she was not feeling well. I was eighteen years old. I took her to the local hospital and we sat in the exam room waiting for test results they had run. When the doctor reentered the room, he asked me to translate some questions for her in Spanish. I obliged. After verifying her age, he restated her symptoms for further affirmation. I translated and confirmed. Then, he asked, "Please ask your mom if she has any reason to believe she is pregnant." I didn't even bother translating that to her. I knew that she and my dad slept in different rooms and fought constantly. It was no secret that she couldn't stand him, so I answered in the negative for her. "No." The doctor was not impressed with my intimate knowledge about my parents' relationship nor satisfied with my answer. He sternly asked me to translate the question to my mother. In an annoyed and sarcastic manner, I turned to my mother and mocked the doctor's question to her in Spanish. *"Que si usted tiene razon de estar en embaraso?"* "That if you have any reason to be pregnant?" As I prepared to tell the clueless doctor, "I told you so," my mother quietly muttered, *"No se."* "I don't know." I stared at her confirming that I heard her wrong and I asked again impatiently. *"Vea! El dijo que si usted tiene razon de estar en embaraso? Que no, sierto?"* "Look! He asked if you have any reason to be pregnant? No! Right?" She looked at me flatly and told me to tell the doctor that effectively, she did not know. Embarrassed, confused and with my cheeks burning hot, the doctor asked me to translate. I did.

Without as much as a blink, the doctor looked down at his chart and informed that, not only was my mother pregnant, but test results estimated she was at least seven months pregnant. He then asked me to ask her if she was aware of her pregnancy. I stood there with my head numb. I was confused, disgusted and furious all at once. *How could she possibly be pregnant considering the circumstances?? Why would they bring another child to the mess they had created? How could they be that irresponsible?* The doctor then repeated the question and insisted that I translate. I searched for the words to translate this to my mother but I didn't need to. As I turned to try to tell her what the doctor had said, she was already weeping. The doctor then proceeded to give her instructions and warnings of the risks about her pregnancy at her age and at that late stage in her pregnancy, but it all sounded like background noise to the ringing in my ears.

My mother was forty five years old the day she found out she was seven months pregnant. I drove her back home in deafening silence as she stared blankly ahead onto the road. When we arrived, we shared the shocking news of our hospital visit with my siblings and my dad. Unlike the standard festivities and celebrations that usually follow an announcement like this, in our household, there was a lot of crying, blaming and arguing that night. My sister and I yelled at both parents for their irresponsibility of bringing another child into the family to suffer. My parents yelled assigning blame to each other for the unexpected pregnancy. The night ensued with useless finger pointing completely disregarding the fact that in less than two months, there would be a baby arriving to this life. I was so confused, angry and frustrated and the only thing I knew was I didn't want to be part of the drama that unfolded there that night. I grabbed my purse, cut through the midst of all the screaming, jumped in my car and drove home to my own place. All the while shaking my head in disbelief and anticipated distress of this poor baby.

A couple of weeks after the initial shock dwindled down, however, we all accepted that there was going to be another sibling on its way but more importantly, we had to focus on my mother's well-being for the benefit of the baby's health. We decided there would be no more blaming or screaming and we turned our frustration into excitement as we began planning and preparing for the arrival of the baby. In very short order, my sister and I decided we would take on the matriarch roles so that he or she would have a better chance at life than the one we had been given. I even reached out to one of my high school friends, Veronica, and asked her if she could help me put together an impromptu baby shower so that I can surprise my mother. Veronica and her mom worked tirelessly helping me plan the party, prepare invitations, reserve food, get decorations, buy gifts, etc. In a matter of two weeks, we put together and executed the most beautiful baby shower we could pull off. Since my mother didn't have any friends, Veronica's mom, who was close to my mother's age, invited all of hers and every one of them showed up with gifts even though they had never met my mother before. The only ones in attendance from our family was my sister and me.

One of the things I remember most about the baby shower, was seeing my mother's face as she laughed and engaged in conversations with the guests as we celebrated her pregnancy. For the first time, I saw her happy, enjoying the company of the woman and smiling most of the time she was there. I felt glad that the party had brought out a side of her I had never seen. Unfortunately, the bliss was short lived as about a month before my baby brother was to be born, my mother and I got into another huge argument that led to her kicking me out of the house and told me I was never allowed to visit them again. No different than our first break up, she again forbade my siblings from speaking with me and no one was to give me updates of the pregnancy. I didn't hear from my siblings for quite some time.

Sergio was born in the later part of August of that year and I missed it. About two months after he was born, my dad reached out to give me the news and invited me back to the secret meetings for coffee once a week. He'd light up describing my new little brother to me and regardless of the circumstances, he was truly happy to have Sergio in our lives. For as relieved as I was that Sergio had been born healthy and everything was okay with him, it absolutely shattered me inside that I wasn't allowed to meet this little person. I wanted so bad to see him and hold him and tell him everything was going to be okay. But my mother would not allow it and my dad had no say in it.

One day, one of my other brothers sneaked a call to me and told me my mother had gone out to the store and he was home alone with the baby. He knew she was going to be out for a while and also knew I was dying inside to meet the baby. So when he called, he said that if I wanted to see him, I would have to hurry before she returned. I dropped everything and immediately jumped in my car and drove like a madwoman in disbelief that I would finally meet my baby brother Sergio. When I arrived, my heart was pounding in my chest and as I walked up to the backyard, I saw my little brother sitting outside on a concrete knee wall with Sergio and was waving for me to hurry to him. I ran up to the baby carrier and wept as I carefully picked him up into my arms. He was such a beautiful angel, and I couldn't believe he was already three months old. I wanted to hold him and care for him and let him know I would be there for whenever he needed me. That he wouldn't ever need to worry about going through the struggles I went through with my family because I would make sure I would defend him, love him and be by his side in any hardship he came across in life. But before I got a chance to dream away my promises to him, my brother, who had been watching out for my mother ran back and nervously said I had to leave. Said that it was too risky and if she came home and saw me there holding Sergio, that he'd be in a lot of trouble. He was nervously rushing me to put the baby back in the carrier and to leave. I had taken my camera with me and I asked my brother to take a picture of Sergio and I while I held him and he did. I then softly placed him back in the carrier and my brother carried him away rushing back into the house. I walked my heavy body back to the car as I cried uncontrollably and drove off. That was the last time I was able to see Sergio until he was three years old.

My high school friend Veronica

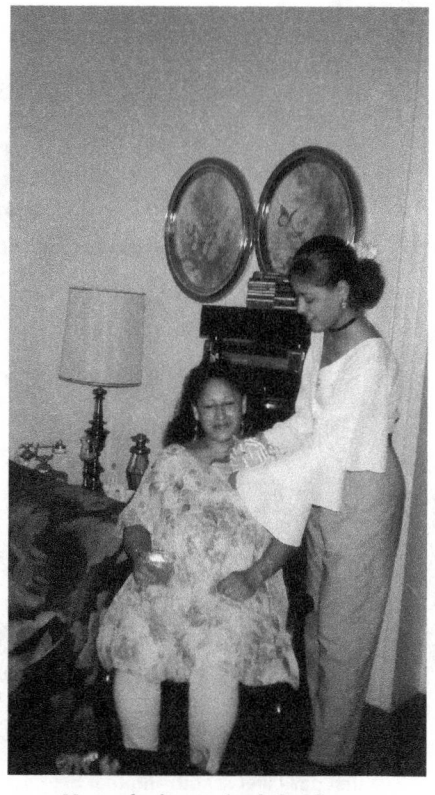

My mother's surprise baby shower

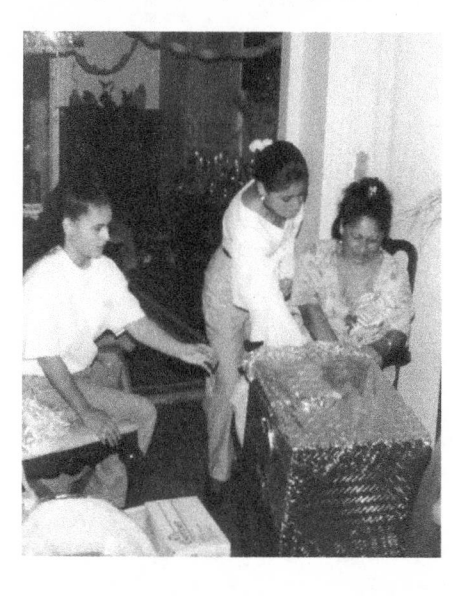

The first day I met my little brother Sergio

# | 11 |

# HAND IN MARRIAGE

*"Do the best you can until you know better. then when you know better, do better."*

**– MAYA ANGELOU**

———⟡———

My life during high school was not the standard life of a young student. While kids my age were going on field trips, attending cool parties or hanging out with friends, I was fulfilling my responsibilities as a roommate, working part-time, paying rent, cooking, cleaning, grocery shopping, etc. which required me to have a very different lifestyle. I had to provide for myself while simultaneously making sure my grades were up to par so I could graduate.

During my freshman and sophomore years, I had enrolled at St. Mary's High School, a private catholic school, where I paid a reduced tuition to attend the school. I had shared my hardship situation with the principal and how I was living with Nuns and she felt compelled to help. However, at the beginning of my Junior year, I was already close to seventeen years old and the principal said the tuition would be raised to the normal rate and at that point I could no longer afford it, so I transferred to the local public school. Elizabeth High School was less structured with a lot more diversity that represented the City of Elizabeth's true cultural flavors. You had students from all walks of life and from all over the world and everyone had their clicks and stuck with them. There were the Colombian groups who you could tell right away just by hearing their melodic accents. You also had the jocks wearing their team bomber jackets representing their school spirit proudly. There were goths, preppies, metalheads, and the misunderstood artists. I identified with the artists the most. Elizabeth was a unique melting pot of its young citizens.

I kept pretty much to myself and only made a handful of friends during those two years. Very few people knew about me or my situation although those who did know, affectionately referred to me as "The Grandma". I liked my anonymity as it was difficult for me to relate to their lives and vice versa. While they were getting ready to go to rad basement parties and drinking binges, I was at my dining table budgeting my income to make sure I had enough to pay my bills. By the time I was a senior, I had worked hard in my dual roles–student by day and employee by night. But I grew tired of the strict regimen I had created for myself with no room to play. I wanted to live a little more like my age group and try to enjoy being a somewhat "normal" high school student while still financially supporting myself. I enrolled in a work-study program that allowed me to go to school half the day and work the other half in the afternoons and evenings. I interviewed with a local law firm and began working as a legal secretary's assistant which provided some flexibility so I could have some time to enjoy my life.

Once I balanced work and play, New York City became my playground. Everything about its vibe made me feel alive! Hanging out in The Village, clubbing at CBGB's, going to underground billiards, or picking up one of the city's best hot dogs at Gray's Papaya at 2:00 a.m. Hanging out with friends while discovering the nightlife became my new hobby and I loved every bit of it. One of my great friends, Josie, who had taken on a role of a big brother to me, invited me out to the city for a birthday celebration of our mutual friend, Mayda. It was to be a group of ten of us and it would be a fun and late night. That night, as Josie promised, was one of the best memories and celebrations I have of the city and of my friends. That night, I also met Mayda's brother for the first time and shortly after we began dating. We dated for about six months and then I moved out of the house I was sharing with my roommates and moved in with my new boyfriend. His sister allowed us to rent her basement studio apartment for a fraction of the going price so that we had a place to call our own. Five months later, I graduated high school in June of 1995 and a couple of months later, after my 19th birthday in August of '95, we were married. He was twenty one.

We got married at the local courthouse mostly because his family, a traditional Catholic family, insisted that we were living in sin by residing together without nuptials. He and I never really saw the same need but out of respect for his parents and his family who had been very supportive and also very adamant about the topic, we decided to move forward with it. We figured we were already playing the role so why not just make it official. Even though I had started speaking with my family again, they did not approve of my relationship and my decision. The day we were married in the courthouse, his family showed up to support us and mine exercised their decision not to attend.

As a young newly married couple, we were trying hard to make ends meet and his parents stepped in to help us out at the beginning. We were so financially strapped that when we got married, his parents had to buy our wedding bands and pay for the celebratory dinner because we were unable to afford it. I had just recently graduated high school and since we moved about thirty five minutes away from my hometown, I was unemployed and looking for work near the new town we lived in. He worked a night shift at FedEx and made just enough to support our bills but somehow we made it work. Our studio apartment was a combination of pieces from garage sales or hand me downs and we shared one car to get around. But even though the beginning was humbling to say the least, it taught us to be resourceful and to work harder to get where we wanted to be.

Eventually, I started working at a nearby mall at Victoria's Secret and we slowly started to organize our life together a little better. I didn't know the first thing about being married but I knew I had given my word in commitment and I would give it my all. I accepted that there was going to be a big learning curve on my part considering what I knew about relationships in my past. This was also the case for him as it was his first real relationship, first marriage and he hadn't a clue what to expect either. But we both knew there was work to be done from both parts and we were willing to do it.

His family and friends became our biggest supporters and welcomed me into the family. They knew some of the details of my past and even though his parents weren't awfully happy about it at least they didn't make a big deal from it and accepted me for who I was. I learned so much about the Ecuadorian culture through them and even traveled to Ecuador as a "wedding gift" from his parents. What I loved most about his family is their closeness and how much they all cared for each other. I had never experienced that before and it embedded in me as an important family value. Even when they had their falling outs, somehow they would all still come together as one and be there for one another. It was beautiful.

He had three older sisters who were married or had families of their own and took me under their wings. The bonus to being in this family was that his oldest sister Mayda and I were already great friends so we got to spend a lot of time together and I didn't feel so "new" because of it. His parent's apartment was always a landing strip of family and friends on Saturday nights. His mom would cook a huge traditional meal and every Saturday evening we would go over to their place and spend hours eating, playing cards and listening to music. It seemed like they always had a great excuse for setting up family gatherings or throwing dancing parties and it was so much fun.

For two years after we were married civilly, his family insisted that the civil marriage did not count unless it was blessed through a church. Again, neither he nor I thought it was necessary but being that his family persisted on the topic, we decided, why not... let's make it official and so we began planning a "real" wedding. I remember going to my parents house and letting them know of my decision. To my shock and surprise, my mother was really excited about the announcement and even offered to buy my wedding dress, which she did. My dad on the other hand, was not happy at all and profusely asked me to reconsider. He did not see the need for me to make such a giant step towards a fairly new relationship and begged me to wait a few years more. I had become pretty defiant in safeguarding my adult decisions without their consent and so I told him I was definitely going through with it.

Our religious ceremony was to take place at St. Anthony's Church. All of his family and our friends attended the service as did my parents and siblings. His cousin, Janet, whom I had become really good friends with was my Maid of Honor. On the limo ride to the church, I stared out the window wondering if I was making the right decision and for the right reasons but I brushed it off to the typical pre-wedding jitters. When I was getting out of the limo, my dad opened the door to help me out and as he did, he had tears in his eyes as he said, don't do it. My dad begged me not to go through with it and said I was making a huge mistake. I remember standing there frightened and wondering if I should listen, but at that point, I had come to terms with my decision and I was going to see it through. No one was going to tell me how to live my life. I told him to walk me in and walk me down the isle. My mother insisted to walk me down the isle together with my dad and so we did. They handed me over to my husband-to-be and as the service ensued, we became officially married.

**Freshman year at St. Mary's school**

**Junior Year - Elizabeth High School**

**With my first husband and my roommates**

**Chavez family celebrations**

**My graduation from Elizabeth High School -
1995**

Church wedding - Family photo - 1997

# | 12 |

## COMING UNDONE

*"The loneliest moment in someone's life is when they are watching
their whole world fall apart, and all they can do is stare blankly."*

– F. SCOTT FITZGERALD

---

It is interesting what happens to your brain when you jam it
up with unresolved memories. You reach a point where there is so
much pressure from unsettled traumas, experiences, and pain that
eventually it all boils to the surface and blows the lid off when you
least expect it.

Late one evening my husband and I were driving home from
being out with friends. I was calm, relaxed, and staring out of my
window mesmerized with the shadows of passing trees along the
moonlit highway. We had a wonderful evening with friends, and I
was ready to go home to rest.

We were fifteen minutes from home, taking the same exit ramp as always. As we circled the ramp, the dark bushes on the right side of the ramp oddly reminded me of those when we were crossing the border. They had never looked like that before and as I squinted my eyes to check them out closer, it was like those bushes brought me back to that awful night. I could see my dad coming out from behind the trees, hands above his head as my mother laid face-down on the dirt and police officers pointing guns to everyone. My heart started racing. The entire border trip slowly started to unfold before my eyes and I couldn't tell if it was real or my imagination. Almost as if I had seen a ghost, I thrusted my head against the headrest as my heart pounded hard in my throat. I felt my chest tensing up, my head began to spin and I grasped for air in hyperventilating. I squeezed my eyes shut and rubbed my lids hard to erase the pictures that flashed before me. The raw pain of the past came crashing into me like a tsunami. My husband took notice of this and knew I was having another panic attack episode. He begged for me to breathe as he rushed to get us home. All I could do was curl up in fetal position in my seat, digging my fingernails into my skin and pounding my chest with my fists hoping it would slow down my breathing. Nothing worked. My face felt swollen, and my tears burned as they streamed down my face. My husband stomped on the accelerator, praying we would not get pulled over as I gripped the door handle like my life depended on it.

We flew into our parking space, tumbled out of the car and down the steps into our basement apartment. We sat at the edge of our twin-sized bed while he walked me through the steps of controlling my panic attack. This had happened many times before and we had figured out what worked to calm me down. He breathed deeply and exhaled, and I followed suit. We would repeat this exercise until I would eventually settle my breathing down to normal. I would then lay my exhausted body on the bed trying to control my thoughts as he would make me a chamomile tea.

His coaching and the tea always helped. We would talk through what triggered my panic attack and through conversation, I was reassured that those were memories from my past, and I was living a different life. After gaining some composure that night, we agreed that I was okay to stay home alone as he had to work the night shift and needed to leave to make it on time. I tucked myself in for the night, and he left to work. I dozed off relatively quick but my slumber did not last very long. I was startled awake by a nightmare I was having where I was reliving the very first time I experienced a panic attack as a ten-year-old girl.

My dad had been beating me with a belt and I was curled up against the corner of the room shielding my body from the lashing. With every whip, I could feel the leather belt straps make contact with my young skin. The belt wrapped itself in snake swirls around my legs and arms creating pink welt marks–marks that I became a pro hiding from teachers and friends at school. As my dad belted me, I recall not being able to breathe and my heart fluttered with palpitations in my chest. I had never experienced that feeling before in my other beatings. I felt too faint to stand up or try to alert my dad that something was wrong. My mother, who noticed what was happening, freaked out and pushed my dad out of the way. She lifted me to my feet and dragged me to the bathroom sink where she slapped water on my face and demand that I breathe normally.

As those memories flashed through my mind, I jumped out of bed and paced the basement floor as I realized that my nightmare had prompted another panic attack. I tried all the tactics my husband and I had used earlier to try to calm down. I tried to control my breathing, I failed. I tried to control my thoughts, I failed. I started punching my thighs to stop the feeling of numbness spreading through my body and I failed. I felt faint and tumbled down to the ground where I lay defenseless crying on the floor. The memories of my youth and years of pain overwhelmed me. One after another they invaded my head. My pain intensified and my breathing became harder to catch. During this most vulnerable moment two phrases came back into my head:

"You will never amount to anything!"

And

"You are the worst thing that has ever come out of me!"

My crying turned into shrieks of pain. I had never felt so alone and so helpless. My chest heaved with dry yelps of hyperventilating pain. twenty-one years of tormenting memories became an avalanche and I lost myself in them. I did not want to be my mother's worst thing! I did not want her to be right and that I wouldn't amount to anything! I hated my life! I hated her for hating me! I hated everything I had lived through and I wanted no more of it! I was useless, worthless and I wanted out! I didn't have any reason to live and I screamed it out! "I JUST WANT TO DIE!" I laid on the floor twisting my head from side to side as I beat my chest with my fists. I dug my nails into my skin hoping to redirect my pain away from my chest. It seemed to work so I violently scratched myself all over my stomach and my arms and started bleeding. I rolled around the floor in desperate agony trying to breathe when I found a sharpened pencil that had rolled against the edge of the baseboard. I grabbed it and started desperately cutting into my skin. I could feel the sharp lead cut into my stomach and my wrists drawing more blood. I eased into that pain and lay on the floor in hopeless surrender and ultimately passed out.

My internal pain had taken me to the darkest moment I've ever been in. I wanted to end my life and all the torment, the failures, the memories, the experiences that came with it. I had never asked to be born into this mess. I had never signed up for the multiple times of abuse, disrespect, violence and scarring I had endured. I often looked up to the skies and demanded to God… *"Why are You doing this to me??*" But that night, I was done! That night, I had enough! I had been sick and tired of being given the heavy rock to carry. And every time I found a freaking place to lay my rock down, I was handed a new and heavier one. My life had been full of rocks I no longer wanted to carry, and no one was going to make me!

When I awoke, the skin on my stomach started to slightly burn as did my arms and wrists. I lifted my head slowly and looked down to my torso to see the damage I had done. I rested my head back on the floor and lay in stillness tracing the path of my slow breathing. I had a sense of disconnect to my body that made me feel at ease and light as a feather. No worries in my mind, no pressure on my chest, no emotion in my heart. Just quiet stillness, lightness, and freedom. I could see what I had done to my body but could not physically associate with it. I enjoyed the numbness of that moment and closed my eyes.

My husband's parents found me. They had been trying to reach me after he called them to let them know what had happened earlier. They were concerned when I didn't respond to their phone calls. They called my husband at work and he rushed home to discover what had taken place... I was taken to the hospital.

Sometimes you must hit literally and figuratively rock bottom to find yourself and your worth. In the attempt to end my life and my misery, ironically, I managed to fail at that as well. But the sliver of hope and light that broke through that darkest moment in my life was what my husband said while I was at the hospital... "You need help. And I won't take you back home until you promise to get help." That night I made that promise. That night I was taken back home. And that night, as I walked back into the studio and looked around to recognize the evidence of my inferno, I knew that I also had to make that promise to myself and I did. That night, I promised I would never give up on Erika again.

Within a few days, I looked for a therapist to help me with my trauma. I went to several therapists and several consultations. Unfortunately, most were awfully eager to write a prescription as soon as I entered their office and send me on my way. Others scolded me for "giving in" to my depression, as if I had the power to control it. Then I found Deborah Patrucker whose name I came across in an insurance directory, and something told me she was "the one".

Deborah's office exuded peace and warmth. Every time I visited her, it was as if my troubles poured out of me as soon as I sank into her couch. Deborah guided me and taught me how to take control of the memories that had far too long tormented my life. Together, and with her careful direction, we created an organized "virtual library" of past experiences that I could revisit with calmness and control. This was no easy task. With each visit, I would conduct a life audit where I had to re-experience every memory, dissect my feelings through each moment, reanalyze it from the eyes of a survivor, and identify the rights and wrongs so I can move forward. That process allowed me to begin to heal and reduce my anxiety. Deborah taught me to store these memories into virtual jars that were placed in my virtual library.

That library represented my entire journey and my story of survivorship. It helped me accept what happened to me so I could grow from those experiences instead of becoming a victim to them. Slowly, through each caring conversation, each assignment to be done at home, every comforting word, I found healing and a sense of self-compassion and empowerment I hadn't felt before. Deborah helped guide me to the peak of believing I was worth saving and in that process, she saved me.

# | 13 |

# LIFE FROM WITHIN

*"Women give life to their children but in my case, my son gave life to me."*

– ERIKA OBANDO

---

By the time I was twenty-two. I had been married for three years and felt like I had made a dent in stabilizing my life. Thanks to therapy, my panic attacks had lessened and my days of randomly losing control were less frequent. Financially we were a lot more stable as we both moved up the ladders in our respective jobs. He had become a Manager at FedEx and I began working for a personal injury law firm in Rahway, New Jersey. Eventually, I was promoted to manage a satellite office in West New York, assisting our Hispanic clientele.

Bergenline Avenue was the epicenter of the Hispanic community in West New York. The block thundered with a medley of music from every Latin country and you could smell the delicious fragrance of churrasco for miles. There were women of all types: the divas who would never be caught dead wearing anything less than a five-inch heel and the matronly ones that swore that matching their hair rollers to their muumuus was just as fashionable. From morning to night, the pulse of this melting pot never ceased to be entertaining. Our office sat squarely in the middle of this merengue party and I loved every bit of it. Even though I spent most of my formative years in the U.S. and identified more as an Americanized Latina, I was always intrigued by and felt strongly connected with my Colombian heritage. I enjoyed immersing myself into my culture and my people while I worked there. About ninety percent of my clients were Hispanic. They would come into the office for updates on their cases and use the opportunity to pry into my personal life, offering endless supply of unsolicited advice. There was always the inevitable question: "Why don't you have kids yet? You're married, right?" I would politely smile the questions away, and change the topic because it wasn't something I had given thought to and wasn't going to do it because of them.

When I was growing up, I didn't think much about getting married or having kids. I was never the one to dream about having a big house with a white-picket fence. Or plan for the perfect dreamy wedding or much less becoming a parent. That kind of life was so far removed from my reality that it never even crossed my mind. My life had been one of extinguishing immediate fires and making sure that the next decision I made, wasn't as catastrophic as the last one. I spent so much of my life in fight or flight mode that planning my later years was never even a thought I considered. I just lived my life on a literal day by day schedule and that worked perfectly fine for me.

Next door to our office was a popular clothing store with a front window full of mannequins dressed in the latest club wear. The owner of the store was the unofficial town gossip, and like clockwork every morning she'd come outside while I fumbled for my office keys and fill me in on everything I'd missed from the night before. In one hand she had her steaming cup of coffee and the other she used to accentuate her stories with dramatic flair. One morning I arrived at work and as she approached for our usual chat, I let her know I was rushing to the bathroom and couldn't talk. I had not felt well all morning. My stomach was acting up, my mouth was watering and my hands were clammy. I made it inside, threw my stuff on the floor, and rushed to the bathroom to vomit. I thought my entire insides had come out, and just when I thought it was over, it would start again.

When I visited the doctor later that afternoon for what I surely thought would be a virus, the physician said, "Erika, you haven't been feeling well because your body has changed. It has changed because it's accommodating your new role. Your new role is a Mom. Congratulations, you are expecting a baby!" The doctor's lips were still moving but I could not hear a word he was saying. *Did he just say I was pregnant?* It took me a minute to snap out of my fog, but when I did, the weight of his words hit me like a ton of bricks. The thought of me being a Mother scared the living daylights out of me and immediately took me down all the memories of what I lived with my own Mother. *Would I turn out to be like her? Was the abusive behavior hereditary? Was I ready to have my own child?* I fell into a full-on self-sabotage with my thoughts and was certain that this would be another inevitable and disastrous fail to add to my list.

The fear was real, and the frightening questions swirled my mind but as the days went by and I sat in deep thought of my new reality of becoming a Mom, I realized I had the choice to rewrite that chapter as well. No different than I had done with my personal life, I now had the reigns to my life under control and knew I could make the right choices in this new role. I made a conscious choice to dissolve my fears and when I did, the euphoria of joy was beyond anything I could describe. I felt that God had gifted me with the chance at making things right. He gave me the gift of life. Not only did I get to nurture a tiny growing life inside of me, but it was a powerful affirmation of my own life's purpose. I now had a responsibility to look at the world with different eyes. I wasn't just going to survive life anymore. I had a precious little being inside unconditionally trusting, relying, and counting on me to plan for our future and all the amazing milestones we would live. That the fight or flight would dissipate into nothingness as I planned our lives forward intentionally. I had reason to live and reason to rejoice. I was going to become a Mother. I was going to have my baby!

I was healthy throughout my pregnancy, but that does not mean it was easy. Despite gaining sixty pounds, I threw up throughout the entire nine months—even while I was giving birth. On several occasions, I had been forced to pull over during my work commute so I could throw up on the side of the road. The vomiting was so intense that my doctor ordered me to stay home from work for the last three months of my pregnancy. By my eighth month, unlike my Lamaze counterparts who loved their glowing look and their perky baby bumps, I was bloated, swollen and tired. But that didn't hinder how much I cherished and loved feeling my baby growing inside me. Especially when it was just the two of us. Since his dad worked nights, I'd be the fortunate one to enjoy when my baby was most active. My belly would morph out of shape as tiny hands and feet pushed out reaching for my touch. I would place my hands on my stomach, touching every little bump and wave, and playfully poke my belly and watch as he would poke back. There were nights I would wake up to my baby's hiccups and I would rub my belly softly until they subsided so we could both go back to sleep. We began working as one without even trying. For nine months, I fell in love with someone I had never met and the bond that grew between my baby and I was so effortless yet unwaveringly stronger each day.

I became more tired and sluggish as my due date drew nearer, but I had a burst of renewed energy the first weekend of February. I cleaned our apartment from top to bottom, my "nesting" instinct had kicked in and was in full swing. My nausea subsided, and I finally had an appetite again. I was in such good spirits on that Sunday afternoon that my husband and I met with a friend for dinner. However, not long after being seated, I felt a sharp, stabbing pain in my lower abdomen and in short order, the pain would return every five minutes. I screamed the entire way to the hospital and shortly after 6:00 p.m., I was wheeled to the delivery room to give birth. We were finally going to meet our baby!

My son was born at 1:00 a.m. on Monday, February 2, 1998 after seven hours of labor. As soon as he was delivered, I started throwing up again, so I didn't get a chance to hold him right away. After the staff quickly helped me get cleaned up, they placed him in my arms for a quick photo and then I passed out from exhaustion. When I finally awoke, a few hours later, his dad was sitting next to my bed, cradling our new son in his arms. I could see his tiny little eyes were tightly shut, his cheeks and lips, a perfect rosy pink and tufts of jet-black hair peeked out from his knit cap. He nestled quietly in his little body burrito as his dad brought him over to me. My heart raced in anticipation of meeting my son. When he was finally placed in my arms, my soul felt absolute. The love, was as new as love at first sight but as familiar as a lifelong yearning. For the first time in my life, I understood my why. This gorgeous baby boy instantly taught me the preciousness of life and made me feel alive for the first time in mine. As he longed for me as only newborn babies do, my mothering instinct awoke and so many things became clear. That morning, when I became a Mother, the seed of real strength was planted in my core because I knew that from that moment on, I had purpose. I knew that having all the answers never mattered but I was ready for the unmapped journey ahead. I would love him, honor him, teach him, and mentor him. The time had come to share the new toolbox of life I had been putting together and my son and I would change the narrative together.

As I shut my eyes and pulled his little face close to mine, I could feel the softness of his breathing on my cheek. And as I felt the tears roll down my face, I whispered my son's name for the first time.

"Hello my beautiful Cristian Andres." I hugged him close as I wept in absolute bliss. I then softly kissed the top of his forehead and promised, "I will always love you with all my heart and I dedicate my entire life to you."

**Christmas 1997 - almost 8 months pregnant**

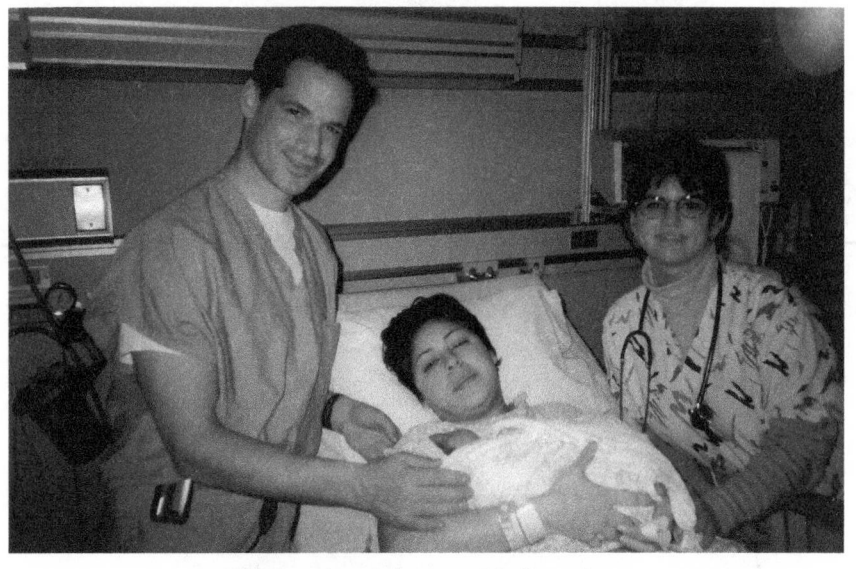

The first picture of my son Cristian and me

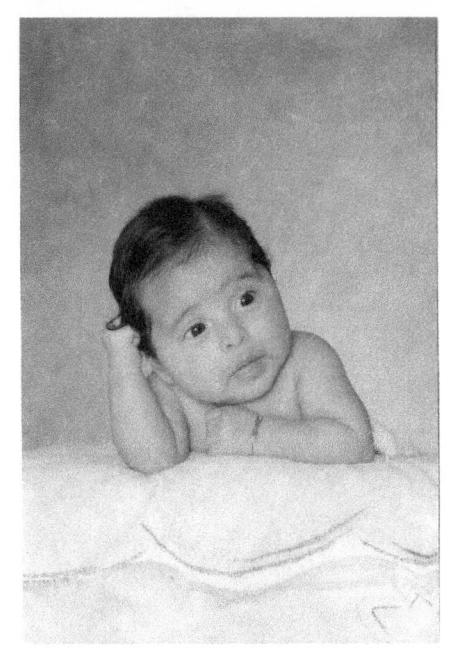

My gorgeous son, Cristian Andres Chavez

# | 14 |

# IN SEARCH OF ME

*"The most difficult thing in life is to know yourself."*

- THALES

---

I had a lot of self-confidence issues growing up and didn't think much of myself as an adult either. The only thing I gave myself credit for was being real good at adopting survival skills with each experience and moving on to the next. In retrospect, I think it was easier to hide behind the excuse of my past than to look deep within to find out who I really was and what I needed to fix in me. Rather, it was easier to devote my time doing things for others, so I wouldn't have to address my own insecurities.

When my son was about three years old and after seven and a half years of being married to his dad, we divorced. We were very young when we met and by the time we grew up inside our marriage, we realized the only thing we had in common was the love for our son. Even though the ending of the marriage was for the right reasons, I desperately still wanted to feel as if I belonged to something greater than my brokenness. About a year later, I met someone whom I fell in love with and in short order, I married for the second time. In my never-ending quest for a fairytale, I brushed off key elements of a balanced relationship, but we still enjoyed an overall good life while he helped me raise my son and we both built our careers.

In the late summer of 2004, while still living in New Jersey, my son was now six years old and I wanted a better place for him to grow up. Despite the trauma I had experienced in Florida with the arrest of my family, I always focused on recalling the fun memories of our time there. Simple things such as the warmth of the sun on my face, the smell of the ocean breeze, and the joy of driving with the windows down regardless of the season. I wanted that lifestyle for my son and my new relationship so we packed our bags and hit the road.

My first job in Florida was as a legal assistant at a personal injury law firm in Boca Raton. About a year into my employment with that law firm and after nearly seventeen years in the field, I started to feel burnt out. I recall one morning walking into the office and plopping down heavily at my desk. I no longer loved the work and I did not want to chase a job or a paycheck anymore but there I was. As I tried to convince myself to start my computer, I heard shuffling at the desk behind me. Another secretary who worked there, whose retirement was long overdue, was placing yet another picture frame in her cubicle. Over the years she had documented every vacation, every childbirth, and every hairstyle she ever had, in photos inside that cubicle. On this day, however, she was frustrated as she could not find an empty space to place her most recent photo, an image of her family who had just been in town visiting. I am not sure why this question came out, but I turned to her and asked, "If you could have done anything different, what would it be?" as I pointed at all the photos around her. She looked at the frame for a moment and then looked at me as if she had been waiting for someone to ask her that all her life and answered, "I would have lived out my dreams instead of all of theirs."

That day I knew I had received a compelling message. Growing up, I felt as if I didn't have choices but as an adult, now I did. And after feeling the heavy weight of her response, I didn't want to have those same regrets. I had been so busy with my head down just going through the motions of existing that I hadn't taken the time to actually plan the life I wanted. I knew I wanted to enjoy what I did for a living without having it be money driven but never really did anything about it. However, after having heard my co-worker's answer that day, I felt compelled to seek alternatives. That night I went home and asked myself, *"Erika, what do you want to be when you grow up?"* My thoughts flooded with career opportunities as I rummaged through diaries and notebooks for inspirations. I revisited old quotes I had saved from speeches that impacted me and then I found my high school yearbook. For my senior year quote, I wrote, *"I want to be an Interior Designer."* I sat on the floor remembering exactly what I felt when I wrote that. I had such different plans in my mind at that age and would have never guessed I would end up where I did. Fast forward twelve years after high school, I was working in a job I didn't like with a forgotten dream I never pursued. There were a lot of reasons I wanted to be an Interior Designer back then. For one, during middle school, I discovered that I had a forte for art composition and it came naturally to me. And when I had my first home, I developed a niche for designing and interior decorating. But I believe my biggest motivator for pursuing the profession was my mother's hoarding. I thought that if I could learn how to beautify a home, it would erase all the memories of what mine used to be.

In 2006 I enrolled at The Art Institute of Fort Lauderdale (Ai) and became a college student for the first time at age thirty one.

I was juggling my roles as a part-time student and full-time employee, mom, and wife. I wasn't sure what I had signed up for but registering to be the first-generation college graduate in my family, considering where my story began, was pretty exhilarating. The anticipation of managing all these roles really freaked me out though as I didn't think I had it in me to succeed. But I kept reminding myself that nothing was as hard as my life had already been. And the picture frame in the cubicle moment impacted me enough to force myself to believe that I could do it at least one class at a time.

Sometime around year two at Ai, I met another student named Lizet. She played an interesting role as she taught me an incredible life lesson that changed my life. Lizet and I hit it off and I was quickly invited to her group of friends. We had a great group of women of all ages that would get together in the school cafeteria to study. There were young girls who still lived with and were supported by their parents and then there were others who had grown children, full time jobs and were finally getting around to fulfilling their dreams--myself included. We even had older women who were grandmas and were hustling just as hard to get the work done as the rest of us. These women inspired me beyond words, but I still instinctively held a cautious distance from emotionally connecting because I felt safest that way.

In grade, middle and high school, I only had one or two close friends and never really fit in with the big crowds or cliques. I was extremely selective with who I let in my life and trusted very few people. As I now reentered the student world, I realized I was no different from that girl in earlier years. I was the type to join in conversation whenever I could relate to a topic but for the most part, I felt more secure remaining in my little bubble of solitude. That rule also applied to engaging in any type of public displays of affection with others. Although I knew how to love and be affectionate with my husband and my son, I was extremely reserved with everyone else. Just wasn't in my nature to be hugs and kisses with other people as I felt it was an invasion of my personal space and privacy. I guess this was a safety mechanism I applied from my childhood. Literally when people would come up to hug me, I would immediately freeze and get very uncomfortable and most of the time, I would avoid the interaction altogether.

One night as we all prepared to leave our study group for the evening, Lizet came up to me in her excitable disposition and opened her arms inviting me into a hug. My anxiety settled in immediately and I stood there nodding my head as I politely dismissed the invite. She smiled and said, "C'mon, you can do it... gimme a hug." By this time, our group had picked up on the fact that there was something going on and slowly started to walk towards us. I continued to nod my head refusing the offer of PDA but before I knew it, she and the other women locked me in a massive bear hug and giggling as they squeezed me harder into them. At first, I felt like I couldn't breathe, and I wanted to cry. I hated the way it invaded my space and I didn't want anyone touching me. But the longer these girls embraced me, and the happier they seemed about it, the more I wanted to let go and eventually I realized it actually didn't feel so bad after all. I never knew what it felt like to have friends want to give you loving with nothing expected in return. I softened my guard and took in the moment. As I drove home that night, I reminisced on that feeling and realized that despite the brassy front I put up to others, it was an amazing feeling to have people holding me and showing me they cared. After that night, I secretly began to warm up to the hugs whenever classes were over and by the end of that semester, I was the one initiating the group hug from all of them. I owe an immense gratitude to Lizet who took the time to teach me that affection, from others, was not a violation of my space but a way to connect at a genuine human level. I couldn't believe that something as simple as an embrace, allowed me to undo some of the predispositions I lived with. When I signed up for college, I thought the only thing I would walk away with was a degree in Interior Design. Instead, I also learned the power of human connectivity with something that started with a simple group hug. Thank you for changing that in me Lizet.

In June of 2012, six years after I hesitantly signed up for college, countless group hugs later, many tears cried, endless sleepless nights, and a book full of awakening moments, I was about to receive my Bachelor's Degree in Interior Design with Cum Laude Honors. I was also asked to deliver the Keynote Graduation Speech to all my graduating colleagues of The Art Institute. As I stood at the podium that night and paused before delivering the last line of my speech, I realized I had achieved the unimaginable. That night was a culmination of hard work, unflagging vitality, and a will to keep going forward long after my mind and body had reached limits. I had believed in myself for the first time, and there I was finding out I had a determined woman inside of me all along, who lit a fire behind her dream and achieved it. That in forcing myself to focus on the day to day goal, I had arrived at the finish line proving I was worthy and capable. And standing before men and women from all ages and walks of life, I was finally adding a new title I was proud of in mine... First Generation College Graduate. It was a moment in my life that made me realize, I had more grit inside me than I gave myself credit for and as I lowered my head to my notes on the podium, I took one deep breath in, blinked my tears away, held my shaking voice together and concluded my graduation speech with:

> *"...I want to leave you with a quote from one of our greatest minds, Albert Einstein, as he once said... "As artists and great spirits, we will always encounter violent opposition from mediocre minds." To this I say, don't let this define you, instead let it fuel you!"*

The graduation party that night was more than a celebration of my achievement. It awakened a woman inside of me that didn't want to just simply survive anymore. I felt that this was just the beginning of an insatiable need to learn more and to discover how far I could actually go in life. My insecurities had finally begun to subside, and I wanted to take on the mission of making a difference for others but also for myself. However, in the days that followed and as I began mapping out the endless road ahead for the next exciting chapter in my life, another part of it was crumbling. After the course of twelve years, my second marriage had settled into deterioration mode when we began questioning our individual identities outside the relationship. As we tried to navigate the process of identifying those crucial voids and differences so we can work through the newfound self-awareness, that marriage ended as well.

**Civil ceremony of my second marriage**

**Last holiday photo with our mini pug**
**Mona-me**

**Six years at Art Institute - 2006 to 2012**

**Lizet and I at an Interior Designers event**

**Art Institute Graduation**

**Cristian and I during my graduation from Ai**

First Generation College Graduate - 2012

# | 15 |

# THE POWER OF FORGIVENESS

*"To forgive is to set a prisoner free and discover that the prisoner was you"*

**– LEWIS B. SMEDES**

---

There is a famous quote that says: "Holding onto anger is like drinking poison and expecting the other person to die." When people hurt us, we get angry, we feel betrayed and most of the time we walk away suffering without properly reconciling our feelings. Some of us carry on with our lives, constantly feeding that resentment and hatred towards the person. And sadly, in most cases, the other person that hurt you is completely unaware of what they did. And as they continue to live their lives perfectly fine, you become the only prisoner in yours.

As a result of my childhood, I spent many years indignant, and I held on to grudges proudly while I claimed to be a victim. I had a deep despise for those who hurt me, and it entitled me to feel sorry for myself. I even sought out sympathy from others because it justified feeding my woes. It affected my friendships, my relationships, and my family as I lashed out arrogantly. I put so much more effort towards finding reasons to seek pity and justify my pain than looking for solutions to heal and better myself. But I reached one point where it got old and exhausting not only for me but for those around me who genuinely wanted me to just be happy.

Most of the anger I was holding onto was towards my family and it affected my every day. I constantly questioned why my parents would raise me as brutally as they did, and I felt cheated out of a normal life. But when I made the decision to forgive them and stop questioning the process, it brought me peace within and allowed me to let go of the weight I carried for so long. I replaced my resentment with empathy as I placed myself in their shoes. They had limited education and resources to apply a different behavior other than what they were taught. Their individual childhoods had been even more hellish than mine, and they were executing life the only way they knew how. I chose to believe that in all the painful experiences we lived as a family, there was an underlying good intent behind it that possibly was corrupted by our hardships. But the most important part of forgiving is being able to recognize that the people who break you, are acting from a deep unresolved brokenness within themselves.

Another significant reason for changing the way I looked at forgiving was because repeating unhealthy patterns with my own child would only serve to cyclically use the broken tools I inherited. I experienced more than my share of trauma and dysfunction and I wanted no part of handing this down to my only son. I wanted to give him tools like love, compassion, respect, discipline and the only way I was going to achieve that was showing him by example. We all come to a place in our lives where we are presented with a choice:

*Do we follow the template we have inherited, or do we have the courage to create our own?* Creating a new framework is never easy but even with the hard work required, that option is the most rewarding at the end.

The ideal way to start the forgiving process in most cases is to speak directly with the person who caused you harm. That way the situation can be discussed, addressed, and resolved between the parties. But in most realities, this scenario is difficult to recreate. For example, I had to learn how to forgive the man that violated me when I was a young girl. Seeking him out would have been near impossible and perhaps even more damaging. But it didn't mean I needed to hold on to that pain either. I had to do the forgiving work myself and accept that I could not change what he did to me, but I undoubtedly had the choice to change how it affected me. I was no longer his victim. I actively chose to become an empowered woman with a voice who invoked respect and I took away the ability for him to make me feel otherwise. The same applies to the relationships I no longer have in my life be it friendships or family. Some of them became too toxic to invite them in to share my life and so I learned to love them from afar and wish them well. I was not willing to compromise the work I had done to be at peace. You must learn to be okay honoring yourself and with choosing who you share your life with and who does not have the right to invade it.

The day I was to reunite and reconcile with my dad, I had put all kinds of conditions on how it would be and what I would allow. I was vacationing in New York from Florida and my brother Sergio had asked me to meet with my dad because he wanted to see me. I said that I would go to New Jersey to meet with him but only give him thirty minutes and then I was off to enjoy the rest of my vacation. But the reality was, when I walked in to the restaurant and saw how happy it made him to see me, and how we were finally able to put the past behind us, it literally felt like he also made peace with that little hurt girl inside. And the thirty minute restaurant meeting turned into seven hours at his beautiful apartment laughing, reminiscing on the good times, enjoying each other's company and looking forward to being in each other's present lives. Fast forward to the last few years, I couldn't picture not having him in my daily life. He brings me so much joy, makes me laugh with his corny jokes and checks up on me to make sure I am good. He adds tremendous value to my life and I couldn't be more grateful for all we have lived through. As we have gotten to know more of each other at this stage in our lives, I also realize, so many of the personality traits people compliment me on, I owe to him. In taking the time to forgive the past, I gained the only thing that matters... my dad in my life.

Another important element is to find purpose in suffering. Believe it or not, my parents inadvertently taught me the most important lessons of my life. Now that I no longer hold resentment towards them, I was able to see how my life with them changed me in positive ways. I learned to be a fighter and to continue the fight no matter how many times you get knocked down. I learned that home and family is composed of those you choose to invite into your circle whether they are related or not. I learned that independence is not when you leave a home but when you find strength in who you are as an individual. And most importantly they taught me grace and courage because had it not been for them taking the risks they took to bring us to America, regardless of how scarring the undertaking was, I wouldn't be who I am and where I am today.

Allowing forgiveness to clean out your heart makes room for the one thing that makes all the difference in the world: LOVE. There are so many people out there who are vested in loving you, respecting you, and valuing your worth. But none of that can enter your heart if it is already full of bitterness, fury, and hostility. You have to do the work as painful as it is because there is no one else that can do it for you. Forgiving is not easy at all. It takes a deep dive into understanding what caused your pain, reliving it and learning how to let it go. And just like any kind of scarring, it takes time so be kind with yourself in the timing of that process.

Lastly, forgiveness of others is worthless if you can't forgive the most important person in your life which is You. For years, I felt I deserved the situations in my life for making bad decisions. The guilt of having failed consumed me. I failed at being a child worthy of love. I failed for bringing pain into my son's life. And I failed for not being the person everyone else needed me to be. But so often we give vindication to others easier than how we redeem ourselves. We are so critical of our imperfections and then wonder why others see us that way as well. Forgiving yourself starts with self-compassion. With a sense of inherent worth despite your actions or circumstances. It's allowing the discovery of self with patience and love and giving yourself permission to be imperfect and make mistakes along the way. That no one was born with all the answers and figuring them out in failures was part of succeeding. In honoring yourself, you find that you will begin to attract those who love you exactly as you are. And nothing you ever do ever merits self-deprecation.

When I began the exercise of forgiving myself, I had to start deep within. I realized that there was still a little girl inside of me in dire need of so much healing and loving and I was the only one who could provide that. I closed my eyes and looked for the forgotten little girl sitting in the corner of my memory that always yearned for a simple hug, to be noticed, to be appreciated and who had the audacity to want to be loved. For someone to look at her and know she had always been more than enough, and her value was priceless. That she was perfect with all her imperfections and her innocence was still intact. That all the chaos she lived through; was not a punishment but a formative base of the amazing woman she would become. When I forgave myself, I forgave the lost little girl inside and now I had a chance to give her all she ever wanted: to be loved. In her, I found the love of my life... I finally fell in love with me.

The little girl I fell in love with

Quick meeting with dad at airport - 2007

Official reunion with my dad and my little
brother Sergio in NJ - 2018

**Painted a replica of one of my earlier pieces
and gave it to my dad**

**Visited with my dad in NJ**

# | 16 |

# TIME FOR A SELF-AUDIT

*"Yesterday I was clever, so I wanted to change the world. Today I am wise, so I am changing myself."*

– RUMI

---

In 2015, my son graduated high school and was getting ready to move into college and start his Freshman year at Florida State University. As I celebrated his graduating milestone, I felt that I had graduated as well. I commemorated the countless days and nights we spent growing together, learning how to navigate life, guiding him, loving him and helping him stay on track to becoming the Second-Generation College Graduate. Now, as he embarked on his new journey, I also found myself embarking on one of my own– being single and an empty nester.

When my son went off to college, I moved into a beautiful apartment, and in my early forties I was going to be living alone for the first time in my life. I had gone from living with my parents, to the nuns' house, to an apartment with friends, to marriages, then single mom. Now, things would be different. My dinners would be a party of one. My evenings would revolve around what I wanted to watch on TV–or whether I wanted to watch TV at all. I had no one else to care for but myself. A lot of questions went through my mind. *What would I do with my time? Would I be nervous or sad to come home to an empty apartment? Who would I talk to about my day?* I was apprehensive at first, sure, but as the weeks went by, being alone turned into an opportunity to get to know what I could be in this phase of my life.

The adjustment to living alone can be difficult if you have spent your life as a caregiver and supporter of others. When you are the key figure in managing the everyday tasks of your family and their lives, your dependency on being needed becomes part of who you are. That's why it's so challenging for empty nesters to let go of their children as they move on or fall into a depression after a relationship ends. Their entities are so fused with their children or spouses that when your care is no longer needed, fear becomes overwhelming. Solitude forces you to finally take care of the one person you know least about, yourself.

One of the first things I did while living alone was to conduct a self-audit. I needed to know who Erika the person was because I hadn't a clue. No different than when I would go out on a date with someone, I asked myself the questions I wanted to know about me. *What do I like to do on my spare time? When was the last time you traveled? What is something I've always wanted to do but never got around to doing?* I then created a list of all those answers and used it as my dating playbook. My weekends became time I spent discovering and crossing off items from that list as I started taking myself out on "dates". My favorite outcome of dating Erika was how it shed light on how many obstacles I made for myself. I was too scared, or too young, or too old or too busy to do the things I wanted. But I forced myself that no matter what I put down on that list, I had to go through with it.

This didn't end with just a list of weekend dating activities. It was equally as important to take care of myself during the week. Each morning before I went to work, I wrote positive notes and placed them on my kitchen countertop to welcome me home in the evening. I wrote notes of appreciation, notes of love and notes to remind me that I was doing fine. On Mondays, on my way home from work, I'd stop at the grocery store and buy myself a bouquet of flowers. I treated myself to a gift once a month of something that I really wanted to buy. And when the weekend arrived, I would dress up and look fabulous for my date: ME!

So often we go to great lengths to give the best versions of ourselves to others but when it comes to looking in the mirror, we are so harsh on oneself and we never merit our own time or admiration. Once I started to enjoy being with myself, I noticed that my happiness became contagious. My thrill-seeking friends would invite me to join in their adventures. And somehow in learning how to love myself, I attracted the kind of man I was meant to be with. I had bought myself a Jeep and so I went on countless off-roading trips and challenged myself to learn mechanics in the process. I started painting artwork again because now I was inspired and had time to focus on my crafts. And ironically, the more I painted, the more my art became representative of my new life–of taking a blank white canvas and turning it into any masterpiece I wanted.

We tend to hide behind excuses of time, of family, kids or work so we don't have to focus on our personal growth. The reality is that we can't be available to help others if we don't help ourselves first. No different than when you are on a flight and the attendant instructs you to make sure, that in case of an emergency, you place your mask on first. You are no good to anyone else, if you don't save yourself first. And no one ever said it was a crime to carve out time to honor yourself. I've had this conversation with so many people and when I suggest for them to go on a trip by themselves, it's quite funny how many of them respond with instant anxiety and excuses of why it wouldn't be possible. But I can't tell you how life changing it was for me the first time I traveled alone.

I made reservations at a cottage over on the west coast and created a tourist itinerary. Everyday, I set out to have a different experience learning about the area. I went to museums, I went kayaking, I built my first sandcastle and, in the evenings, I BBQ-ed for myself or sat at a restaurant alone and met new people. That was a phobia I overcame. I had always been afraid of sitting alone at a restaurant or bar. I avoided it to the point where I would rather eat in my car then sit alone at a place. But I changed that the day I challenged myself to dissolve that fear. And just like that example, and during multiple vacations alone that followed, I spent time breaking down so many hindrances I had. And at the end of those trips, I came out a new woman.

There's a quote that I found during my finding Erika era, *Become the person you want to marry.* We have a laundry list of qualities we look for when we are in search of a partner. He must have this, and he must do that, and he must make me happy. But have you ever thought of becoming that person and possibly attracting your significant other that way? We don't think like that. We are bred to expect and demand what we want instead of becoming who we want to be with.

Relationships, love, parenting, they are all based on this theory. Getting to know yourself so much and emitting that confident energy is what makes people gravitate towards you. I'm sure you have friends who you can only take in small dosages because they drain your energy. And there are others that you can't get enough of because they elevate you. Use that as your personal gage. Which of those people are you? And is that the same person your friends and family think you are? And whatever those results are, make the appropriate changes. Ask the deep questions of why you are the way you are and then pivot to what you want to be. Be the type of contagious energy everyone wants to be around with. But more importantly ask yourself, *would I want to hang around with me?* Applying good discipline and focus will get you to be everything you set your mind to be. I promise you! Love who you are, and if you do not know who that person is yet, create your dating playbook list, take a trip alone and go find out.

Cristian's High School Graduation with Honors

Taking time to center myself and my mind

Trying new adventures with my son

Rekindling my love for painting

Accepting the challenge to learn mechanics

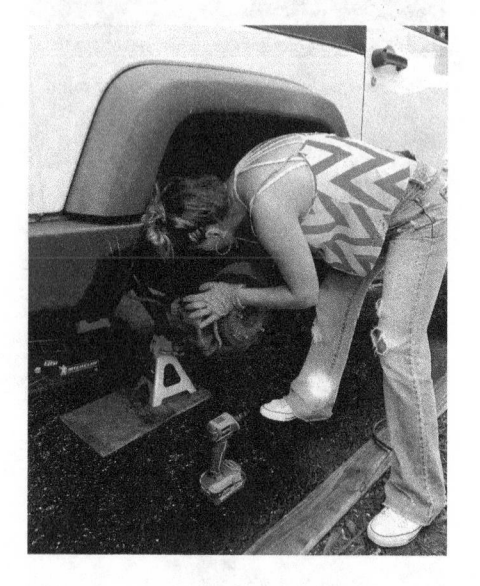

Fulfilling a dream of becoming a Tedx Speaker

# | 17 |

# A WALK IN HER SHOES

*"To be a woman is to be unapologetically resilient despite every-thing."*

– H.H.

———— ❦ ————

I shared my entire story for the first time in public in front of a group of twenty women. One of the founders of this women's group and my dear friend Maria Cristina, who knew of my story, convinced me that it was something that needed to be shared with others. I was so nervous and was not sure what to expect from it. I thought maybe I could possibly enlighten one of them, or if nothing else, they would certainly be entertained with listening to the crazy journey of my life. But I certainly did not expect it would have the impact that it did both on them as well as on me. I spoke for about an hour or so and after I was done, all of the women stood up from their chairs, applauded and then lined up in front of me. As they came up to me one by one, some shared their own stories of resiliency, some without saying a word just hugged me tightly as we cried together, and others thanked me for giving them inspiration and hope. We had all connected so deeply to pain, to happiness, to survivorship and to our hope. But in the energy of that connection, we all opened wounds in our memories that needed healing. One of the women, a natural healer who specialized in trauma, engaged us in a meditation to make sure we didn't leave the event with opened wounds. She walked us through a guided exercise of hugging the little girl inside of each one of us and let her know she was loved and cherished. It was one of the most amazing resolutions I've ever been a part of. Even more important, that day I realized that my story wasn't just a story. That my experiences had tremendous power to connect on multiple layers with so many people that have also been hurt in life. It gave courage to those without a voice and that day, I decided I had a responsibility to continue to use mine.

I've since spent the better part of seven years sharing my story as a public speaker on multiple stages, platforms and countries. When I do, the purpose is to help others look at their hardships as opportunities for growth and inner strengthening. Because it's within our deepest pain, our hardest hour and our moment of solitude that we find out what we are truly made of. It's where we find self empowerment and resiliency. Our stories make us who we are. The moment you can see that, you find yourself and your purpose. You weren't born into this world to pay bills. You were brought into this life to leave your unique mark and legacy!

We all come from a story. Mine wasn't any easier or any harder than the next. It was simply the story I lived and became a better person because of it. I collected many lessons throughout the years that I turned into the tools which helped me rebuild myself. But more than that, I continue to build a legacy for my son, for the generations that will follow in our family lineage and also help as many people as I can who cross my path and need a compassionate hand. I believe that everyone deserves to be freed from their self-contained mental prison and be guided into knowing that we all have the right to change the ending of our stories if we just believe we can.

A while back when I was doing research for a speech I was asked to deliver; I came across a very cool video on the internet. It was a video of a white table and someone placed an ant right in the middle of it. The ant began scurrying all around and about the table. Then someone drew a circle around it on the table with a black marker. As the ant reached the black line, it would kick back away from the line. Then it would try to move in another direction just to find the line and kick back again. Suddenly it had limitations. It was no longer free to roam about and now it accepted its confinement within that drawn circle.

We are no different than the ant. We are born free souls with so much to discover, so much limitless creativity and then circles are drawn. Family, friends, spouses, society, social media, they draw these lines around us, and we accept the limitations of those boundaries without question. Whether the boundaries are real or not, we go up to those lines that refrain us from being who we are meant to be and we retrieve back into our insecure selves. We are told we are too big, too small, too ugly, too pretty, too quiet, too outspoken. Someone will always have something to say about you. Sadly, most of the time those opinions are merely smoke and mirror reflections of their own fears. Not yours.

Here is a piece of advice... Push through the lines! No different than knowing that if the ant were to just go beyond the drawn lines, the limitations would cease to exist. The same applies to you in your life. You know who you are. You know deep down what you are capable of so tap into your own source and make of your life what you want it to be. Not what others demand you to be. If I had believed all the times I was told that I was not capable, you wouldn't be reading this book right now or the ones that will follow. I had to come to a lot of places in my life where I made an active decision to trust that the yearning inside of me was worth the fight. Furthermore, when I lacked the spirit to follow the calling for myself, I did it for the one person that deserved it the most, my son.

Today, my almost twenty three year old son, Cristian, now a distinguished college graduate, is my greatest pride and none of my achievements will ever come near surpassing the accomplishment of having raised him. Seeing as he goes about his adult life reaching for all the possibilities this world has to offer, I recognize a familiar fire from within. His ambition to make a difference resonates with all the days and nights I instilled in him that he mattered. That his VOICE mattered. That everything he set his mind to do, he would achieve if he fought hard to believe in himself and worked even harder for it. To recognize that in the discomfort of growing pains, he would find strength and purpose. As he exemplifies compassion, love, understanding and integrity, I know society has received an incredible human being that will contribute in extraordinary ways. While he stands before others offering his hand to help, I know he is intently leaving a legacy all of his own.

We all have a choice to become who we are meant to be regardless of age or what happened to us in our past. If ever there comes a times when you can't find the ways to believe in that, quiet your mind, reach deep within and tell yourself there is a fighter in you that is ready to show you what you are made of. Remember someone once told me I wouldn't amount to anything and here I am proving that prediction wrong and becoming living proof that all is possible when you believe it to be so.

Strong people come from tough circumstances and it is up to you to decide how your journey will ultimately define you.

My first speech for the women's group

Speaker for Women Empower Expo

**First International speech at the World Happiness Festival in Mexico**

**Tools for becoming Victorious - Excuse Me That's My Seat
Conference**

**Cristian's Graduation from Florida State University**
*Photo by: Andrew Salinero Photography*

My son, My Friend, My Life

With the late Dr. Wayne Dyer in Fort Lauderdale

With Maria Cristina who helped me share my story

*Photo by: Linzi Martinez Photography*

# ACKNOWLEDGEMENTS

---

There is no shortage of words to express the appreciation I have for all those who made this book possible. I am so grateful to the friends, and family who believed in me, guided me, and helped cheer me along this project for the almost three years it took for its fruition. Your wisdom, support and love are immeasurable.

Cristian, God gave me the greatest gift when He blessed me with you as my son. You saved my life when I had lost my reason to live and my love for you is so profound, it's embedded deep within my core. You are my entire world and the reason I live and breathe each day. No different than the first day I held you, you stole my heart and I've never been the same since. Thank you for the countless memories of enjoying the good times, sticking together through the bad times, all the laughs, the wrestling bear hugs and living this wonderful life together. Papa... I love you with all my heart. Please remember that no matter where you go in life, I will always be here supporting everything you ever do! You make me so proud to be your Mom and you'll always be my little monkey.

Dwayne, my *"Mantequillo Bello"*, words cannot describe the love I have for you, what you mean to me and the impact you have had in mine and *"Pinguino's"* life. You are one of the most resilient, loving, giving, and selfless human beings I know, and I am forever thankful that my prayers were answered with you. You've inspired me, motivated me, and loved me like I've never been loved before. Thank you for your never-ending patience, support and for making me feel so damn invincible. I have you to thank for starting me on this path of finally writing my story when you whisked me away to the fishing camp. Three years ago you helped me set the stage on a quiet beautiful beach so I can type the first pages of this book and wow... here we are. Thank you for crying with me, laughing with me, living life with me and for having the little boy in you, take the little girl in me out to play. You are my home.

Dodie, had it not been for the amazing Leo that you are, I'd still be struggling to finish editing this book. Thank you so much for grabbing my hand, running with me and helping me cross the finish line. But even more important than that, thank you for inviting Cristian and me with such loving arms, to be part of your beautiful family. Nothing comes close to creating the memories we do with all of you and I love you all very much. *#LoveDoes*

Thank you to the friends that through thick or thin are there whether to wipe away tears, raise a glass in cheer or help me steer. Anne Reinstein, for always picking up the phone no matter what is on the other side of the line. Thank you for your friendship. My dearest Brittany Momah for being the incredible shining light that you are and for all the great memories we lived with you. Thank you for always sharing your huge heart with Cristian and me. We love you! Robert Butterfield for extending your hand every time I needed it and for being such a caring and funny friend. Wilmar "Alex Shell" Gonzalez por siempre ser ese hermano amigo fiel que me inspira todos los dias a sonreir, a darle gracias a Dios y gozar plenamente de la vida porque solo tenemos una. Dayana Maya and Ena Hughes... thank you for always being there for me when I needed it the most and supporting me without judgment. I'm beyond grateful for your friendship all these years. Thank you Yulia Konovnitsyna for being such an amazing and contagious energy and for inspiring me as much as you do. I admire the wild, adventurous and courage woman that you are and I hope to one day have a fraction of your bravery. Tia Marta and Freddy, for always welcoming us into your home all these years and making Cristian and I feel so special. Thank you for creating such wonderful memories together. Alexandra Flugel, for being born on the best day of the year, my fellow August 1st Leo. Your mentorship and friendship have meant everything. Thank you all with a humbled heart and love each one of you!

Sister Filomena of Hogar Nazareth, Diane McMillan, School Counselor at Elizabeth High School, Debra Patrucker, Clinical Social Worker, Tammy Berman, Mental Health Counselor, My Counseling Connections... you all helped me at different stages of my brokenness throughout the years of my life and taught me to believe in myself. I owe my sanity to you.

The late Dr. Wayne Dyer – Philosopher / Author / Speaker. Dr. Dyer's documentary "The Shift" completely changed my perspective of life. His teachings, his books, his videos guided me through my awakening age and to my path of seeking a life with purpose. Meeting him in person a year before his passing and sharing a meal as he bestowed priceless wisdom with me in 2014, was a blessing that motivated me to work even harder to answer my calling. Because I know you are listening... Thank you!

I want to say a very special thank you to all my friends, co-workers, bosses, acquaintances, fellow speakers, authors, and life coaches who taught me countless lessons of authenticity, perseverance, and seeing beyond my circumstances. It would take me years to list all of you by name but you know you hold a special place in my grateful heart and I thank you for becoming part of my story and my life.

To the readers of this book, thank you for taking your time to read my story. I hope that within it, you found tools and nuggets of hope and inspiration to help you begin your own journey of finding purpose and a road to healing. If I can leave you with one last gift is to please remember that you are the most important person in someone's life... Yours! Believe that you are worth the fight every step of the way because you are!

*Photo by The Wedding Traveler*

Erika Obando - A relentless advocate for defining a life with purpose, Erika has made it her mission to leave impactful ripples for generations to come. An active International Speaker, Author, Mentor and Community Leader, her legacy is to guide others in changing the narratives of their lives. Her efforts focus on women empowerment, youth enrichment and advocating lifestyle pivoting using the art of reinvention.

She took the renown TEDx Stage in which she shared her story - "When Breaking Points Lead To Empowerment" – a look into her life's journey of resiliency and perseverance. Using her own story's success as the platform, she teaches the tools of transforming yourself from being a Victim to being Victorious!

Website: www.ErikaObando.com
Facebook / Instagram / Twitter / LinkedIn
Email: Erika@ErikaObando.com
Kindly please leave your book review on:
www.Amazon.com / www.BarnesAndNoble.com / www.GoodReads.com

CPSIA information can be obtained
at www.ICGtesting.com
Printed in the USA
BVHW040450140922
646850BV00004B/13